THE
ANNOTATED
"HERE"
and
Selected
Poems

THE
ANNOTATED
"HERE"
AND SELECTED
POEMS

Marjorie Welish

Coffee House Press   Minneapolis

Coffee House Press is an independent nonprofit literary publisher supported in part by a grant provided by the Minnesota State Arts Board, through an appropriation by the Minnesota State Legislature, and in part by a grant from the National Endowment for the Arts. Significant support has also been provided by the McKnight Foundation; the Star Tribune Foundation; the Lila Wallace-Reader's Digest Fund; the Bush Foundation; the Target Foundation; General Mills Foundation; St. Paul Companies; Honeywell Foundation; Patrick and Aimee Butler Family Foundation; the law firm of Schwegman, Lundberg, Woessner & Kluth, P.A.; and many individual donors. To you and our many readers across the country, we send our thanks for your continuing support.

Coffee House Press books are available to the trade through our primary distributor, Consortium Book Sales & Distribution, 1045 Westgate Drive, Saint Paul, MN 55114. For personal orders, catalogs, or other information, write to: Coffee House Press, 27 North Fourth Street, Suite 400, Minneapolis, MN 55401.

www.coffeehousepress.org

COVER + BOOK DESIGN Kelly N. Kofron
AUTHOR PHOTOGRAPH © Star Black

Library of Congress Cataloging-in-Publication Data
Welish, Marjorie.
    The annotated "Here": new and selected poems / Marjorie Welish.
        p. cm.
    ISBN 1-56889-098-5 (alk. paper)
        I. Title.
    PS3573.E4565 A8 2000
    811'.54—dc21   99-088965

10 9 8 7 6 5 4 3 2 1
first printing / first edition

for Joseph

CONTENTS

THE ANNOTATED "HERE"

CASTING SEQUENCES (1993)

THE WINDOWS FLEW OPEN (1991)

TWO POEMS (1981)

HANDWRITTEN (1979)

ACKNOWLEDGMENTS

American Poetry Review: "About the Length of an Arc"

Bomb: "H Is for Hat"

Colorado Review: "Empired Illumined"

Conjunctions: "Corresponding Saints"

Denver Quarterly: "Chronic Dreams," "Michelangelesque," "Nowhere More Vivid," "Of a Display," "Suppressed Misfortunes"

fragmente (Oxford): "Still Life," "Thing Receiving Road"

Grand Street: "Fingerprints"

Lingo: "Look, Look!," "Touch Me Not"

New American Writing: "Crude Misunderstandings," "Opera," "The World Map," "Thing Receiving Road," "Vocabularies"

New Observations: "False Isle," "The Black Poems"

Parataxis (Brighton): "An Exit Throughout," "Exclusive New Feature," "'Hasn't She a Ticket?'," "Macbeth in Battle"

Sulfur: "At Table," "Collaborating with Materials," "New Preface by Author," "Preface," "Preparing a Length of Arc"

The World: "The Annotated 'Here'"

Acknowledgment is made as well to these anthologies: *The Gertrude Stein Awards in Innovative North American Poetry* (ed. Douglas Messerli, Sun & Moon Press) for publishing "The Annotated 'Here'"; *Out of Everywhere: Innovative Poetry by Women in North America and the U.K.*, (eds. Maggie O'Sullivan and Ken Edwards, Reality Street Editions, London), for publishing "Situation" and a selection of previously published poems.

Some poems appear in French translation by David Mus in *Po&Sie* (ed. Michel Deguy).

The author would like to express gratitude to the University of Georgia Press, to Burning Deck, to Z Press, and to Sun for permitting publication of a generous selection of poems.

THE ANNOTATED "HERE"

THE ANNOTATED "HERE"

The Annotated "Here"

The here of actual space, addressed
in face, to face
proximally yet aesthetically in pencil
like an eyelash

an eyelash addressing the canvas
which tantalizes.

                    And so forth.
"And so forth," meaning "setting out"
reiteratively from the heartland.

The here throughout actual space addressing
your face essentially in pencil
like an eyelash acquainted with the canvas's
indolent pressure.

                    And so forth.
"And so forth," meaning "setting out"
reiteratively from the heartland.

The throughout weave
of face essentially

the weft in pencil
abstaining from canvas.

A parallelism
of focus and of setting out
permitted us this facility.

Gravity

1.

Where would public space do it? Do for it? Itself slowly
descending into thing and he who died ignited deep enough,
cinder block of commonplace
assignment comes into view.

Gravity and the second
turnstile of reinforcement and extinction . . .
extinguish only to reinforce the eye,
grammatically:

gray advance in sentence
cinder block in assignment of four enclosures multiplied by four
comprehensive offering of closet hypothesizing scale; and far
figure along enterprise

within the tasteless lab
that constituted understanding tries the object at hand.
A hand will divide into three parts
of apprehension.

2.

Cinder in a plaza is better than
pumice in a palace.

3.

The intent "of the gray color" or "tending toward gray"
creosote of "flesh-preserving" length

was lost on the hollow blocks. "Nonetheless,
'foundation' was the word most frequently used" at the grave.

"Of the gray color" or "tending toward gray"
at the corners belonging to that body . . . , or notice this tendency

4.

toward gray: a thorough and sustained analysis of the gray scale
slowly assimilates all language.

A Work

1.
Left of the median, deferring,
right serving the same silhouette:
the silhouette of taking half,

then half again, within
a box, siring box-like
textual symptoms most widely speculating

on a set of fixities
consumes prestigious amounts
of interchangeable nature

reliably modular
weighing in modular
dimension

of fixed lust
characteristic of the exterior
boxes in series

even as much of this ballast
anticipates interior
diction.

2.
Box, divided from self, expects orienting louver.
(Note the mortuary practices sustained.)

Two pages—the isomorphism is only partial, of course.
Falling short is a prospect of a kind.

Two pages from afar, "of the two malefactors who were crucified . . . ,"
"We now follow the second procedure," he said.

3.
Exterior dimensions invariable
interiors variably unthinkable.

Exterior dimensions invariable
interiors variably thinkable.

Artificial lakes
artificial lakes

to the left, to the right
ordination of the interior.

This Near That

Imagine a logic of like size
arresting exteriors, even as interiors are restless

skeptical, or defective relative to use
as a reservoir, aqueduct, or kiosk.

"A small simple sheltering or enclosing structure."
A locale requiring a lid is logically incomplete.

A definition of pluses
"and occurring in multiples" readily modular

if verbally reconfigured, may be reconfigured
as follows: "a structural reduction in answer to Tatlin."

Across a wall is a something
Something designates a wall.

"Something having a flat bottom and four upright sides" is a delegate
of sets of descriptions. Our professed subject.

The Open

". . . something having a flat bottom and four upright sides,"
for we have emptied the statuette and spent most of its childhood
extension. "I asked him if he were pleased to decompose,
for the thousandth time, a violin . . ."

of aerospace. Interior increasingly studious is twice
seen, once in profile, once in profile re-routed
to the interior, where is assumed
red, a quantity of it.

"This Hit That" and the Like

We are pointing to that, to make mention of the new world, ostensibly
of the new world, ostensibly an answer to *Corner Counter-Relief.*
"Not that one. *That* one." In plywood, very heavy evidence.

Box, public collection and box, crushed possibly when wet.
". . . visible universe which is not the basket," texts.
You see it whole, intractable: first phase of apprehension.

Pointing to "that there," we name it "bin" whose height brought about
disruption of the box by deepening the rationale.
"Five is a number while 'five' is a numeral."

Translations of substance to "that there, that one"
or "bounding line drawn about" the funerary basket in stone, a new objective.
As death, so "untitled." Name one

rainbow—unmistakably apparent stimulus.
We name it "bin," to speak of "five" in decline.
Can room be found? The founding of landscape.

"That is beautiful" in aluminum, confined, however to the face
that did not fit any system and so passes through his heart.
"Passing through his thin heart" is a reference to "pan."

Speaking of substance, we mention "thing" as a pseudo-concept.
Read "this" as "recurrence of this" in this landscape of facsimile
and column. In some system, landscape and chimera are interchangeable.

At Table

Of being suitable
or to the right of the fold,
$\qquad\qquad\qquad$ extrapolated
like this, like that intelligibility
of plate fettered to table, with program,
academe in hand, and denoted forks speaking with us

transitorily . . .
$\qquad\qquad$ "Scattered totalities,"
$\qquad\qquad\qquad\qquad\qquad$ live knife
put to glass and the future of us in words
for which a reasonable defense might be given.

To the right of the implied dish, place emphasis:
$\qquad\qquad\qquad\qquad\qquad\qquad$ come and attempt

a fine thing:
the drift of place setting iterated as a landmark
of the new school
attaining to non-aligned subject-object relationships.

You ask for a pledge
or sleds to barter for intensities, as plates being adjacent
bestow similacra in the manner of "winged words."

Of winged words and dwindling likeness, you are saying:
the pen is on the table;
$\qquad\qquad\qquad\qquad$ come and attempt

"a sentence of the glass-on-knife-on-dish variety."

A Project for Aspects

As chair is to table, so hair is to fortuitous
interpretation, we have said in selected
nonsense. As dinette of miniature instinct
is to "dinette set," it is night in whichever octave
chairs face inward to promote pitch dark
aspects correspondingly affiliated with furniture.

And inverted kitchen chairs apparently
indicate someone is about to close the restaurant,
or to strike the restaurant. A special talent for referring
is fair of face. Four chairs distractingly
false may or may not lie
face down to become aesthetic by definition.

A chair overturned: buyer beware!
A thorough zone and hereafter
instancing vernacular homelessness
of chairs pulled across the tiled floor
of things we know to other subsequent
works in a domestic setting

littered one side only. A fragment of clientele
all took chairs, then assumed chairs
under the vast ceiling fresco,
to initial the paper that appeared to be
taking advantage of the surface of the unspecified table,
the occasional table, in phrased shade of a chair.

THE
WORLD
MAP

The World Map

Prospect in readiness, together with
the annexation of processes,

                 revealing—dissembles

landslides or pure lyric
by which to complete the fragmented prayer "as intended."

Dumping gravel
               on emancipated frontiers . . .

If H.B. really were
darkening a bildungsroman of irony, he would say of R.R.
he is second,
            that he is the second most interesting philosopher,

or that the tenderness of located
skimming stones
             across pain and dust

"helps us get what we antecedently decided."

A landslide
          idling in the mirror . . .

Crude Misunderstandings

Hair dyed black signifying the dogmatically youthful . . . ,
and the evidence of intent

                                    falls through the concept
in Picasso's rendering—

a kind of ultimatum of the much-extolled chiaroscuro
falling against the nose.

A torrential chiaroscuro to be thought about
or thought with:

                        as the intentional digestive of planes
contrariwise, her head opened out
                                    like a parking garage.

Or a ruler with an orb.
A commandment no less unconditional

        than pervasive space.

Call the space cloven by any distinction
axiomatic. Dye it black.

A vacant lot makes things pleasant.

Vocabularies

Patina correlated to pattern
Mark overlapping mention
                          simulating much.
You said,

Mention is not art, despite
much mention of suffering simulating
                          abrasion
of canvas—no—
                not "of"
in the sense of "belonging" or
"integrally the business end of a rake."

You said,
Rake raking gravel,
racing gravel, a gravelly race
her precursors never knew.

You said,
Paraphrase
              at cross-purposes to abrasion

through use. Abrasion signifying use
once your receipt had been utilized as that
rake incarnate
              changing the subject.

And the noise is kept alive
through the tatteredness of mass and time.

Opera

It will have been
                              phrased in tauromachy
to cause people long-lasting pain.

Pulp and paper, the embodiments.

And in our restatement, in the scraped surface which
infuriated the subtle theorist,
                              mention is
growing pale as death, mention is enumerated.

It might have been
                              "the rubbing together of membranes"
in faces modulated through demonstrable use, tempting you
to agitate for
                              the right-hand edge left free—
and beneficial leaves.
                              Improving intelligibility, he moved further away.
By analogy, the rational cosmos.

To agitate for wax
                    which when rubbed
                                                  as antihistamine
                    and most prolific spacing
cherished use
                    of beautiful yellow gold
prefigurement of beneficial chemistry.

It will have been a serious pursuit by aerial railway
swirling toward him.

                    An elevator raised by twelve columns
inscribes a place within a system
                                        of urban agora
and superlatives sailing into our harbor.

Later we shall annoy our plants of heaviness, of lightness,
and we shall slide the gate of the contemplative elevator to refer to
something
purchased
            in a pleasantly static pursuit of experience.

Preparing a Length of Arc

In the space of barely
indicated hospitality is Vico tasting his forks,
and his gutturals,
with uncommon interest in "undifferentiated matter."

Prepare to enter. Prepare a number
or a letter
in shame, culminating in
canvas through the left-handedness of
the orthographic. We must enter shyly, as in "I have no idea,"

The hand in estimated area makes a vast "B."
Its biceps are backwards, and we are apprehensive
toward modern phraseology, specifically the phrase "B and B,"

doubling breakfast.
                    Revolutionary guidebooks
attempting "Bed and Breakfast" (which I heard as
"breakfazed"), bring exaggerated light: your bed is the bedroom
when empty; emptily your bed would play the tyrant.

What is the notation for such expressions? A specious present
the very craving of which may be "B *or* B"—

                                        there must be something
referred to by such expressions.

About the Length of an Arc

Weighing left-handedness on the canvas,

                              Demonstrably yours, Cy.

He let the line drop. He said: "Imagine that we have
straightened the wire without stretching it."
Below it, a number that may measure the wire
while abstaining from it.
                    In basic idioms
of boundlessness, the canvas invites writing
a number in abstinence,
or as though "out-to-lunch," which is a sure sign of
inward boundlessness in Vico,
                        who is elsewhere
taking his forks, yet also and fundamentally, taking his fork
with his left and transferring it to his right
in his children, his commitments.

Of language and the prelinguistic
left-handedness and "vocalissimus" at its source, he had something to say,
would have apprehended the difficult fixative in the words "speak it."
Speak right-handedly, he advises.

"If you ask me, that thundershower is through-composed."

Meanwhile analysis grew and grew
in the baby. "B" and then "B" and then "Brr."
With performative scratches and eventual socialization, left to right,
the roaring wind. The wind in vagaries
let us stutter further
                    for a wealth of
usage: more analytical when left-handed than he seems in ratiocination . . . ,
reversing "B" in time
to rest our conceptions.
You left your watch to wind down.

                    Pa-pa!
From the lips of bed, P rolled out a beginning, drove a thundering hangover
from bed to earth. "May one begin where one pleases?" he asked.

"Look, Look!"

"Look, the birds have freed the Stop signs."
—Robert Rauschenberg

Eyeing Wilson's lecture on Eva Hesse is as an expense
rather than a liaison . . . ,

where the life-force of Kyrie Eleison lay in pursuit.
While words may point to hallucinatory greenery . . .

. . . only to learn she had happily reassimilated the attire of ruffled feathers
native to France, for ruffled feathers as

endgame amuses them, ruffled
feathers happily ever after.

The ideology of self-possession, "in ellipsis rather than a full stop,"
intervenes artistically at this level.

"It's impossible?" A little too administrative
for me. Your opinion,

together with the two annual newsletters.
N.Y. Birdcalls for Övyind Falström, circa 1965.

Ugh! Aargh! Oh. Oh, Anna, you could address us.
Who were to pass? Conferences of hosannas, and your help as well.

Helllp! We would appreciate your help in opening our columns, Palladio.
Thus, it seemed necessary . . .

Writing of zones in non-contradiction, or protocols columnar and in confusion,
you could address us.

Ruffled feathers exciting, agitating protocols,
oh, confusion!

AN
EXIT
THROUGHOUT

"Mommy, do you want to see me run fast?"

                                        "No."

An Exit Throughout

Or a ball around which it is not raining
in everyday language. The word "is"
consists of three letters.

                        Leaving this arrant
inconsequentiality, and diminishing

                                in the mountain light by a factor of three
is the word "is."

It is not raining.
It is snowing.

Exclusive New Feature

Altostratus typescript.
The sky is cloudless: "I have added nothing."
"It is my perception that . . ." as a kind of prophylactic for lying.

If yes,
enter brief miracle.
I have added nothing
a priori blue.

Once again, the satisfactory
has overtaken Cape Hatteras. It will be a pleasant upset from the once
possessed mob. All
into words:
"Hasn't she a ticket?"

"Hasn't She a Ticket?"

Doesn't she appreciate a ticket? POSSIBLE WORLDS ARE STIPULATED and
doublestruck, she, in duplicate on a short road.

"I can't."

Islands without prior written consent

envious of empty islands

in dimes that

consent to "NO" sonorously.

When is a door not a door?

A door

"NO" unmentions the latest scholarship, hinged to reduction
or contradiction. Or contradiction in droplets.

Nothing moves. Envy. "I can't." Isles of contraries

as envy

is to hope.

Aestheticizing ethics as in marble

is lettering insofar as "HOPE" proffers "*ENVY's*" italicized "*E*" etcetera,
improving the other's "H" through doubling. Or by having doublestruck hope
enviously, or by envying hope's stasis, inscribing it notoriously, on the
breasts.

Extremists in marble notorizing "HOPE," and "*E*" having been
inscribed in pestilence to whisk across "H" in bed.
HAVING TAKEN THOUGHT UPON DEATH

plunges us

into non-contradiction exactly, more interestingly-paired incommensurate
antinomies creating beautiful truths, no?

Legendarily all-purpose: Bachelor Crossing. Liking hope and linking
it, a theological virtue, with a cardinal vice.

"Rarely, if ever"

is flat. What do you mean: a *good* book?

Fingerprints

Two lower buttons notwithstanding

                                —not true

both views at once.

                Posthumously.

"Scaled to a lady's hand," *op. cit*.

                          applicable to any practical

matter.

If this were the case, they suppose something like

                                   eyewitnesses in the

remote

interdisciplinary popular culture, or, The Limousine in Art, to appease
an interest group, although
a topic is not a thesis,

                knowing each aspect,

                             an immense rock.

Fingerprints, thirty and humiliating,
of which we are not shown enough, posthumously, apply to
the subject,

              in haste.

                    On each person's card,

the skin system.
"It has to be supposed there is an internal norm which maintains
the," he said,

              (without naming them)

                          lines on thumb

about reasoning and serendipity in the subtableau.
"Hence, D is the thief."

Line Drawing

A lost center
We lose the center to
                              a short step.
Lose center to gutter until the labyrinth is
no longer an explanation.

The construal lay low, no one
could find it in the fold.
                    What cannot be taught or resolved in
memento of victory.
                    Sticker, pin, pen, flag, a flag lost twice—
                                                    the entire
gamut of left and right luffing, and a person believes it.

Not-*p,*
        a lost center.
Lose center to gutter until the labyrinth entails loquaciousness.
Supposing this.

A person believes the labyrinth to be seriously absent.
Lose center to gutter, skeptically.
                    . . . is worth mentioning
                                        which horse . . .
A specified method has persuaded you.
A flag, a flag provides strong evidence.
                    A flag lost
the entire garment of left
and right that philosophers will admire, or would evidence in

100% location,
            the corner store being considered prime
somehow made to be understood:
                    Did the dog . . . ?
definition
            sticker.

"When the horse was led from the stable, did the dog bark?"

Macbeth in Battle

"Let's get married." "That's False."
"Not unmarried," she estimated.

Redness is whimsical or whitened. "I wonder
where my wallet is?" is not a question

but an implicit temptation trafficking
in interrogatives. Adam and Eve

encumbered.
              Between languages

subsisting on value, and modernism.
The idea of gray is not a true copy.
                                "Don't!"

as a bridle for packages intimidated
amid prehensile pathways.

"What's the manner with you?"
                             "Ready, or not!"
if you rotate the letter "N"

in your dialect of mathematics. And on a dark night,
bridle, strap, leash, vanilla, are celebratory.

Imagining vanilla, the reliable confection
luckily aestheticized, we are tempted to say,

chasing ethics
after surgery.

Using clues: it is raining, it is not raining. Do not eat
                                        knives frozen.
"Excuse me?"

Do not eat peas with a knife, knives.

                                 "Excuse me?"

          In brain areas,

"RAW" in neon
making "WAR"—

             or else!

                    Physical interference

yet non-contradiction
mentions why.

Chronic Dreams

A function of x
foreshadows
"of" with "less"
in an impaired crossing

of arithmetic processes,
while a number greater
than a portfolio of bathers
destroyed

takes the product
of two numbers greater
than "of" and very stimulated,
in an effort to do the wrong thing

for the right reasons:
saying "of" when naming "less"
until amnestied. For the right reasons, he gave
the tablet a spatial location in haste.

Situation

                              Failing this zig-zag (composed of
smaller zig-zags), while chaotic,
are properties "less necessary." Nevertheless,

Nevers is failing part of his chest
                              running out of the house
sequentially. Non sequitur made by that.
                              And she

whose syllables went saline, is unthought
or thought to be between mental states,
through which a sieve through which she drew a sieve
of disinformation,
                    pamphlets, and etc.
                              (Subsequently repeated
tryst, heavily indebted
to a wall or to a wealth of adjacent method
for her whose personal history went saline among the pharmaceuticals
and sometimes tearful.)

And sometimes these seeming advantages fade
into face that is harbinger of extraneousness.
                              Face related to a
lack into which a naturalism casts a few
                              —the film is about the lack
of map, of mapping German onto French
fixity of the sign, through which reading himself satisfactorily went
into overdraft.
              Unthought to be between mental states.
                              And she,
attributing locutions, kept after.

Of a sequence unthought through a sieve
of disinformation
                    in paper, half a mind to
                              up-end pocket money.

Negativity, the architect of,
would have something discontinuous to say.

Touch Me Not

Let me introduce . . . do you know Joe Brainard? If not,

why not?

If he is as finite, as bound to time,
a small mass of dripping paint . . .

"I don't . . ."
"I don't . . ."
"I don't . . . what?"

"Don't touch the wood."
"Don't touch—cut. Don't cut the wood."

As he is finite and bound to a bed,

speak after me:

"If the wood is too long, okay?
If the wood is too long, make a cut, then make a second cut."

As an émigré neighboring on time yet abominable
let me introduce or express something
of a complaint: you want.

"Young or old?"
"For that I don't need English."

COLLABORATING
WITH
MATERIALS

Collaborating with Materials

1.

copy, move, delete; ventilate, waltz, drench, mention, gesticulate
stapler, page, ream, work, envelope; word, sentence; subtext
foot, wrist; through, across, beyond, beneath, upon, underneath

Underneath sentence, breath deletes self-addressed stamped envelope.
Apparatus, valorous though it may be, does not ventilate word.
Surplus of white structuring element beneath surface is asparagus.
Flush asparagus with sponge. Tap water flush left.

Insert brick in life.
Insert syllable in life, black ink only.
Immerse book in ink-flushed syllables, ink-fleshed syllables.
Borrow terminology from rainwear.

Delete mercantile subtext in the insurers' phrase "earthquake resistant."
Multidimensional thunderstorm finds off-putting
beauty in paperback.
Underneath book is lack proportional to longish brick.

Euphemistically-surfaced tablets mention sentences, surplus of vacuous credentials.
Dusk-surfaced tablets immerse angel.
Mention "angle-irons" and the chill assumed in the box.
Disciplinarians fasten many if not most syllables to the table.

2.

Perspiring star
that comes to rest, is understood as coming to rest
on the surface of space, stapler gesticulating

wrist erased, reappearing in subterranean mention.
Ream somewhere must reckon with afterthoughts
of perspiring star

of perspiring star rooted in page
prior lives rerouted eccentrically throughout the apparatus
in consequence of afterthoughts, in which the last sentence is the same as the first.

The teacher of Alexander permitted it.
We remember the stapler ventilating the text, which we erase
even as apparatus explains it, stratospherically.

The work was then signed pseudonymously. If our star is
perspiring, it is owing to the bricks just drenched with breath and word.
Necessarily valorous subtext

says joy from drenching bricks through the wary
apparatus of hoop
on the court in consequence of stratosphere utilized to the utmost,

and owing to extra stratosphere he dished out,
our multibreasted star.
Detailed exegesis would then become

a radiant obstacle
that validates altering the course of stratosphere, surplus of white
structuring elements beneath surface—stones

which address foot, district of foot.

Preface

Underneath quarrel
lies racecourse.

Estates throughout and unmarked are reached by no crossing
in purgatory, an expression of an unmarked state.

To make it adequate, okay, not more than once,
less than one is to mark naught.

Naught else but naught ventilating
height and not more than this faktura.

Width of something . . . yet less than two, severely unwritten.
Several erasures greater than one unwreathe it,

it unwritten umpteen times in splashes
canceled through severance,

canceled through cat yet compensatorily tempting
naught cat throughout crossing, and not one

canceling stamp. Several of them unwreathe it yet
in treachery: one, the unmarked not hitherto in contract.

New Preface by Author

Underneath quarrel lies space
audited in cockpit.

Estates throughout and unmarked and reached by no crossing
in purgatory, an expression of an unmarked state

adjacent to valise. Naught ventilating
aggravated ivy where adequate.

Visa in purgatory okay not more than once,
less than one is to mark naught

minus valise. Naught else of the proleptic
and not more than this faktura.

Valise greater than one yet less than two, severely unwritten
several erasures greater than one unwreathe it.

It unwritten umpteen times in splashes
canceled through virulent delta

canceled through cat yet compensatorily tempting
naught cat throughout crossing, and no inverse

alternating current. Several of them unwreathe it yet.
Arithmetic everywhere, with a little text.

H Is for Hat

Regrettably, you put it near me.
It was as though an unstoppable fact had come between us.
How appropriate, therefore, to be literature in a bereft state,
unpaginated.

You were sorry at every level, perpetual, conceptual.
You were sorry. No one speaks here. That we are speaking the same
language oozing incomplete arithmetic
would be nice. Put it next.

"To throw with an overhand pushing motion"
to put the shot
to plant or imprison or formulate the shot—
"I am talking, by definition, about *it*."

Putting a finger on Ecclesiastes
in other possible worlds, possibly your world of warmth and cold
easily magnetized,
reclaims it, it and other assets up in the under-eave space.

Corresponding Saints

The floor's countenance
distributed throughout social consciousness.

"I no longer know" is not the same aphorism.
"I know." An aphorism

advancing neither . . . nor.

The floor-through element in Anglo-American . . .
the floor-through Anglo-American element in verse tribute.

Prone floor apart from texts
prone floor *folded like a napkin*

or the ideogram of *Noh*
with the resultant *planes in relation*

advancing neither loquaciousness.

Flourishing dialecticians do impart juggernaut.
One hundred thousand dialects substantiate it.

Flora enjoy that milieu of ground and sky
and sky and ream of paper decreasingly.

We won.
We did not win.

The house was not unoccupied.
The house was occupied.

Flora initiate intrinsically burdensome ream
of boasts and insults called pleasing.

Empired Illumined

Drape the empire in obstacles, neon
lamps, while with closed eyes, occlude heavenly
electronic instruments and the python

in repose. Adjust the draped neon
worked loose from the assembly
hung on the artist sinking beneath the maelstrom

of lights. Place python on referendum
requiring approval by July
in gorgeous patience and semiperiodic ruin

to reinvigorate its themes. Draft python
for this purpose. Drag physical substance. Lay body
of the emperor amid the irreducible selves of neon

to reveal the massive calm of the referendum
entering code. A succession of moves, severely
old music in skeletal form

contending with underestimated maelstroms,
is said to describe self-similarity,
in a necropolis heaving mighty neon
or adjusting preset electronics that work the python.

False Isle

Resilience had expressed some isles
and disappeared, as it were, into the false
commitment of a provident file

cabinet or an edifice of aisles
postulated faultlessly
in the auditorium. These isles

of annihilated numbers are ill
with vapors. Subsumed doors, false,
hypothetical, and filial, adorn the *Isle*

of the Dead by Arnold Böcklin. And why
this esoterica of all else?
this henceforth rusted tranquility? An isle

carpeted in aims and methods, declaring aisles
in sawdust, as though to propose false
mantles. Illegitimate lights and filial

incisions stray across the faun,
threatening the theater of important idleness
that foreshortened literature of our isle
sufficient to lips of a vase, finally.

IN
TRANSLATION

THING RECEIVING ROAD

Still Life

Of address, or else
slow to be

secreted in Tennessee,
is a jar preoccupied

with arrest,
hence placed. It is

fermenting place
secreted and shaded,

is intentionally petitioned
at a time of implicative possibilities.

To perceive is to intend
habitat and plaintiffs,

hence to place
hence to place Hecate

excavated Hecate
placed thee in judicial thought

nets thrown into the water
yet might be meant.

Finders keepers: Roman coins in and under talons
(we are disturbing the earth to get at them).

Jars in Translation

Placing a plate on slovenliness
like a gate to want, accelerated,

the fast litter of pine needles visits a bowl
like Zeno slowly grabbing the wrong sister.

The fast litter of pine needles swelling a bowl
assumed to be non-empty.

Losing a sister like a gate to want, only to find
divine slovenliness disclosed

in the ventilation. It is spring
and we detect it.

To be at a loss meant to place
want at the eye, and to find it there.

A sister arbitrarily close to zero
will ante up impairment

and benefit of hurt. Of related interest
is a theory of prose meant

to blemish a tarpaulin with focal points
apparently, intending the resuscitated rubble.

Rendering Mien

Spilling mien through wilderness, this, after interval.
A mien near wilderness, an increase of mien.
Demeanor near tarpaulins, and that jar.

That jar in requiem for wilderness even on a fingernail.
Mien rubbing itself against folded tarpaulin: folding mien
outside domain, place asleep; place, crossing a fence.

Place of two witnesses, and near, place of the first-born.
Jars spilling wilderness, wilderness as yet not tithed.
Near and far are jars unverified, jars of private language.

Participating jars and tarpaulins are proximate.
Tarpaulins tangent to jars lie there.
Jars in section nearly spill.

Diametrically-opposed tarpaulins spill a wilderness.
Jars on the horizon, tarpaulins at hand.
A wilderness equidistant between a jar and an aspect of a jar.

Thing Receiving Road

1. To lose a place to or allocate a glance
2. (lost, stochastic, and/or both altitudes, of which far or deep
3. disclosure is the missing mass) is to place the place.

The place setting between thing and work
". . . stimulus meaning of a very unobservational . . ." 45, biased the clearing
toward disclosure; the poetics of seeming disclosure (we have cited)
sets upon earth or its buried representation.

"To place" is to refer to
experiments on earth, then to subtract
the predicate, then to move several gracious modules . . .
The wilderness has partially digested the diabolical jar.
". . . untoward nature." 45 To compensate for a welter of win, place, show
I read everything on nature and then anything
with the word "N"—I mean . . .
Rephrasing a logical expression
by substituting "Vermont" in the set, the earth is ". . . inculcated
through other sentences . . ." 45; we are going to fix it.
Identify at least two places where the author
so enjoys places to eat, places to stay, that he writes himself in.
They said they liked the place very much. They found

a packing crate
drying plausibly.

Thing

Where whereabouts wherever here in this place in this vicinity somewhere
aboard at home hither to this place in that place and such
surroundings back home here and there in various places

acquittal for all discursively acquired unity
deluge positing the object
incapable of making the most elementary locale.

One of the words escaped my mind.
What significance has this for the sentence?
An ahistoricity of remembrance is not contradicted.

THE BLACK POEMS

Black Diluvium

nothing deduced
from

black diluvium
quitclaim

sullen through oil
color

drained of gray
matter.

The Black Boxstall

nothing deduced
past

the black box
stall

porous with oil
gas

floating black
hens.

The Black Box Camera

nothing deduced
past

the black box
camera

glacially plastic
with air

emitting pocket
valor.

The Black Box Camera

nothing deduced
from

the black box
camera

polychromed
near

(and blindfolded
by) foxes.

The Black Box Camera

little initiative
asked/unasked of

the black box
camera

flushed by fire
hydrant

in hairless pocket
malodor.

Black Diluvium

little initiative
asked/unasked

of black
diluvium

flushed by fire
hydrant

past stigmatized
ferret.

CASTING SEQUENCES

Twenty-three Modern Stories

Perpetually roughed up
by the dawdling, blushing drone of an airplane,

"the viola with a restrained, sometimes" restringing
made the plunge
upon these planks
because of all the shores that must be visited.

". . . and continuities, whose intersections"
spreading hot wax
on privation
and on the phrase "this text,"
united once again,
are inescapably drawn toward the open door.

The bells have ceased altogether.
"The air bit hard and cold"
spaced in such a way as to make a triad
of arrangements thus:
old and tired star, guitar and protean
interdisciplinary soprano.

Casting Sequences

A page dramatically estranged, nor lacking

                                         bombardment out of sync

with the event that

                annihilated into sudden pianissimo

a few songs.

           Where death is naked to the waist

in radiance,

          and sudden extension

piloted across a vocal line

                finds an event,

the page lies still, a chaotic catchall of springtime.

Alphabetizing the cards,

            slavishly

the person comes first,

          in cold blood

and spelled out . . .

          "pale and enfeebled by the remoteness"

of actuality.

         Of actual number, pale

and spelled in cold,

          a person is imperturbably

alphabetizing cards

         torn from himself,

casting from himself riddle and raven,

                  riddle and reticule.

Mildew

      "of adjacent realities"

and recurrent themes

           and recursive themes,

assisting the physics of a sinking fastball or aerodynamic

stall—speculative,

         half-visible—and all talking at once,

the only such televised
                              obliquities in which
the elite and public are exactly coincident
                                        lifted up.
To get livelier, to
                    accelerate the unridable lift,
the only such televised praxis, half-visible
                                        breaking pitches
wince—
              and they all remark on it,
                              they all recur
in the slower moving air.

Design, with Drawing

1.

And slowly, Monet underwent a conversion from wrist
to shoulder and thence to the ambit
of paint dragged across surface unappeased:

                              plasticity without an appointment
or trace of retinal light.

Unimpressed, an editor asks, "Was Pollock even seen
standing before this canvas opining 'Monet,
Monet, ceasing to exist, I want to paint like you?'"

Apparition. Really, I swear it.

                    And wearying.

And slowly. And somewhere other than observable water.

2.

                    A mossy bank, schoolgirlish

Of lacunae passing through literal mentalities
a few pages later.

                    A parapet, an undercurrent

of misplaced exactitude these odysseys transcended.
Why ask the artist? Ask the art:

                    rock-ribbed

breakwater, to mark the hue and cry of forgetfulness
and gray areas.

Addressees,

what constitutes evidence in stylistic transmission?
Disbelief "much bigger and faster"

                      or problems corroborated,

in a more efficient axe.

Kiss Tomorrow Goodbye

1.
Among us are those who apply
dysfunctional tactics to convened ordinariness
of setting, as in certain booby-trapped stories.

For similar reasons,
a narrative complete with lunch menu and stereoscopic thugs . . . ,
complete with cigarette yet for all that a narrative clad in itself . . . ,
or a ventriloquist and dummy, minus the ventriloquist . . . ,
all threaten the logical unit.

Complete with cigarette
yet disturbing the infinitesimal trash, the depiction,
this ventriloquist set a bowler-hatted dummy
on one knee, served up a twin
on the other.

      Thus translated,
and torn limb from limb, "naively,"
the rivers ran
and Osiris spread showering selves, showering down
existence after death.

2.
Death served up a twin
the rivers ran
limb from limb
trash the depiction
minus the depiction
as in certain booby-trapped stories
for similar reasons
narrative clad in itself
on one knee
on the other
convened ordinariness
complete with cigarette.

Moses und Aron

Entirety.
Inquiry.

Sunken revelation
minus the idolatry

and bacchanalian click-track:
where is ought?

Schönberg asks of this mien,
of this cabinet

impaired to shed light.

Entirety somehow annulled
qualitatively through inquiet,

optimum warmth. Anathema
corresponding to gold

mimesis,
mind. Where is rival

dumbfoundedness?

The entirety hammering outside
the fool.

An appeal to
sounding that note.

You were omniscient a moment ago.
To beguile many and be beguiled by one

incompatibility.
Why?

Schönberg asks.
Screams, laughter, silences.

Do you wish to escape without saving this page?

Dumbfoundedness?
discolored now in laughter.

Screams, laughter where there is enigma
or the onset of the nearby, discolored now,

disinterred many times as they parody ultramarine,
the sun, the sun's disappearance.

Move What? To Where?
Unimaginable, omnipresent, eternal,

stay far from us.
Move What? *Staff, law; serpent, wisdom.* To Where?

Now this God can be imagined.

Scalpel in Hand

1.
Let us effect a moratorium on things.

Let us say
an object is not an image, aerodynamically speaking.

Let us say
"Speak, or be silent."

Let us legislate
"the sound elements in a spoken language."

For argument's sake,
let us say the craze for black
may be dazed with shape, size, and color of commodity.

For argument's sake,
the flutter of nearby bleeding does not render a charcoal lemon tragic,
although tragedy eclipsed by subject matter
may be eligible for illustration by Grandville;
"an object is not an image."
Say the subtly bled shape does not induce suffering in lemons, however
blackened, however centrally massed the putative anguish.
Let us legislate anguish,
let us say "anguish" in unison very loud.
In a spoken language, syllables are extinguished
once gathered by the silhouette dissembling death.

2.
In the center, rays from the sun and much still life
denied body, denied pantomime
and yet much language whenever and wherever

land radii. Abstract and sanitary bodilessness.
If no evidence, if no physiognomic
ignition, then just what does the author mean?

In conversation with the author, find
a charcoal axis drawn soto voce, denied body,
denied yet blurting out unjustly perishable

sacrifice or contingency,
much ostension of cipher
and rays of the sun.

3.
An object is not an image,
aerodynamically speaking.
Verblessness in space
reserving passive
rather than active
tawdriness of those sparse
accoutrements in free fall.
In this falling through representation,
object and image:
snails versus "snails'
genitals in the form of stars,"
depending on how we construe
the symbolic
vanishing magnitude.

In vanishing magnitude,
the symbolic.
Depending on our construal,
stars in exhaustion
and genitals suspended on a string.
Ephemera, illustrate this.
Free fall, illustrate this,
scalpel in hand,
in an acutely skeptical reading
of the snail incised with dotted
passivity in tawdriness,
the object obsolescent, abject, or gone.
When is an object not an object?

Michelangelesque

Only our noon *or my tired breath*
Of ruined evening *or the evil hour*
Named by rival *light to my pleasure*
Defends morning *in frost and shade.*

Perpetual morning *drives out the shadows;*
Contracts, letters, *and the other plume*
Of ever-executed noon *carry within*
These signatures of *consoling Heaven.*

      □

Fire took no thought *or my tired breath*
Wet that day *or the evil hour*
Denying firelight *to my pleasure*
With rain lost *in frost and shade.*

Hurled earth *drives out the shadows*
Unrolling mares' tails, *and the other plume*
In which wake of earth *carries within*
The non-finito, air's *consoling Heaven.*

      □

Air unembellished *or my tired breath*
Stagnates: infanticide *or the evil hour.*
Therapeutic *light to my pleasure*
Unlikely in self-disclosed *frost and shade.*

Saintly utility *drives out the shadows*
Of specious good *and the other plume*
Lit confusingly, *carried within,*
Down from your pedestal, *consoling Heaven!*

Suppressed Misfortunes

"Suppressed misfortunes have a double strength."
—Michelangelo

Breath tired my or *or my tired breath*
Hour evil the or *or the evil hour*
Pleasure my to light *light to my pleasure*
Shade and frost in *in frost and shade.*

Shadows the out drives *drives out the shadows*
Plume other the and *and the other plume*
Within carries *carries within*
Heaven consoling *consoling Heaven.*

◻

Breathing out *or my tired breath*
Hour unpalatable *or the evil hour*
Himself his abacus *light to my pleasure*
Or muddle, tonal *in frost and shade.*

Driven shadow *drives out the shadows*
Ephemeral bounty or *the other plume*
Carries within *carries within*
Contentment, *consoling Heaven.*

Lacing unraveling *or my tired breath*
The problematic *or the evil hour*
Thread, threading *light to my pleasure*
In frost. I, *in frost and shade.*

A system of knots *drives out the shadows*
Almost to a man. *And the other plume*
Unable to die *carries within*
A sampler in cirrus, *consoling Heaven.*

◻

These intervals *or my tired breath,*
Fallow throughout *the evil hour*

Of spirit. *Light to my pleasure;*
Light to my labor *in frost and shade.*

Design *drives out the shadows.*
Visibility, status, *and the other plume*
Of similar worldliness *carry within*
The sumptuary unction of *consoling Heaven.*

□

Of information *or my tired breath*
The merely literal *or evil hour*
Ordering and insouciant *light to my pleasure:*
Verse, incurious *in frost and shade.*

Astonishment *drives out the shadows.*
Of facticity *and the other plume.*
Or is it conception *carried within*
Incessant meriting, *Consoling Heaven?*

Of a Display

Restoration *can be all boredom and anxiety,*
artifice *the only remedy.*
Cast *among us there is nothing human*
alive. *The heart, the mind, the soul will then*
cleanse *the evil of all error*
and *the first and the second death drive out*
resemblance *in my fate.*

Restoration botched *can be all boredom and anxiety.*
Plexiglas broadly discussed *the only remedy*
cast *among us; there is nothing human*
alive. *The heart, the mind, the soul will then*
become more apparent, if not elaborate. *The evil of all error*
and *the first and the second death drive out*
material somewhat feigned *in my fate.*

Ut pictura poesis *can be all boredom and anxiety.*
Euphronios Plexiglas, *the only remedy*
piecing the vast schematic *among-us-there-is-nothing-human*
mixing bowl. *The heart, the mind, the soul will then*
liquify *the evil of all error*
with commentary: *disdain and anger*
belonging to a sphere as *the first and the second death drive out*
the literal mind.

Continuous service *can be all boredom and anxiety.*
Non sequitur *the only remedy,*
and with plastic *among us there is nothing human.*
Leave without pay. *The heart, the mind, the soul will then*
exchange *the evil of all error* for plastic armature,
leaving behind these volutes of *disdain and anger.*
In faulty semesters *the first and the second death drive out*
unceasing surface. Refocus this controversy, enclose.

Repairing the whole *can be all boredom and anxiety:*
support beyond pretense *the only remedy.*

Of the supplement *among us, there is nothing human*
supplying the heart. *The mind, the soul will then*
disrupt, not echo, *the evil of all error*
and toward any but difference feel *disdain and anger.*
Cast from elsewhere. *The first and second death drive out*
historicizing lip and foot *in my fate.*

Faux marbre *can be all boredom and anxiety.*
Museological augury *the only remedy*
for lost material—*among us there is nothing human*
restored. *The heart, the mind, the soul will then*
imitate this material inadequacy.
The evil of all error cannot fail to impress.
Disdain and Anger eating a peach.
The first and the second death
drive out natural phenomena *in my fate.*

Clay things *can be all boredom and anxiety,*
plastic infinitely recumbent, *the only remedy.*
Among us there nothing human
. . . *the heart, the mind, the soul will then*
not sire sense impressions . . . *the evil of all error*
. . . *disdain and anger*
. . . *the first and the second death drive out*
symmetry *in my fate.*

. . . *can be all boredom and anxiety*
plastic sepulchre, *entirely his . . . the only remedy*
. . . *among us there is nothing human*
. . . *the heart, the mind, the soul will then*
. . . *the evil of all error*
. . . *disdain and anger*
. . . *the first and the second death drive out*
. . . *in my fate.*

Krater, I

Plastic,
a voiceless chassis
from which material has abstained
remains uncorrupted by plausibility,
vying with clay
that *returns and returns*
yields as if lowly, portable
dolor and pain.

Even before it breaks . . . *can be all boredom and anxiety*
skeptically at odds . . . *the only remedy*
own lips unexpectedly broken . . . *among us there is nothing human*
insofar as . . . *the heart, the mind, the soul will then*
posture . . . *the evil of all error*
was never so endowed, in doubt . . . *disdain and anger*
. . . *the first and the second death drive out*
. . . *in my fate.*

Krater, II

In its boughs,
historical effacement expending much effort
of classicizing, in clay *for thy dear beauty*
in clay-colored parody,
without deceiving yet without spark.

Is . . . *can be all boredom and anxiety,*
the museological . . . *the only remedy*
problem is that of surmise . . . *among us there is nothing human*
to complete . . . *the heart, the mind, the soul will then*
. . . *the evil of all error*
intentional . . . *disdain and anger*
. . . *the first and the second death drive out*
norms . . . *in my fate.*

Pre-echo

> *Pre-echo:* Sound recorded so loud
> that part of itself may magnetize adjacent windings

Twelve, thirteen, for two came wheeling down,
thirteen, for two darted about your eyes

interpreted as not knowing. A surname
is silenced. As in "tall, if sudden groves"
or as in "scuttled, sudden, and tall,"
interpretations sewn into the unknown are those

we cannot substantiate. Physiognomy centrifugal,
Indo-European murmur gathering the sail
of the kind sailboat there, Igitur.
Mouth and ear are in centrifuge and unquiet.

Unquiet mouths would give more faithful
rendering of dissemination;
dissemination, ever an almost
perverse pleasure in translating tongues

in miasmas to the ear, through the ear.
Mental lakes close and correlated,
green lakes of filial piety
surely of, with, and through the ear.

Torn from the ear obediently
this pieced entirety, in sepia
and insentient, a piece of which
lake is correlated to the ear.

A piece of the puzzle, rotated and blank,
in light pain,
the weight of existence
rotating the blank island,

chafing against the flesh inscape
of unjustified seeking.

Bleak notation for nostrils lower left
in regard of that flesh estuary

pressed from pulp and paper
for a perennial alphabet of lesser mortals—
primarily a thing to be read, you decided.
Select the size and face of type,

in 12-point figure-landscape, all exile
in these islands: dressed
companionable islands, dressed in phenomena.
Eclipse, exiling fullness. Irremediable,

irremediable solitude which constitutes a man.
Every visage, metalinguistic;
unblinking lakes in vague visage stretched across stretchers
which constitute a man.

Unblinking non-mimetic lakes taped to the cheek,
and here physiognomic truth-functions inhabit
a logically scented and non-specific
self vindicated at all four corners, a kind of facial site.

Adrift in such skin, our iteration,
our iteration with which countries cannot vie, transliteration
    secretly abetting impenetrable baptism.
Portents of Rome, is this itinerant baptism abetting ours?
Adrift is the handkerchief

of which the paternity is known,
albeit threaded with thoroughly perplexed reference.
That blotted tongue, that thoroughly bollixed signature
    perplexing an anteriority
we cannot substantiate, this, despite known paternity.

Thirteen, for two darted about the eyes.
And the contingencies were attuned if irreducible;
attuned, if irreducible. And yet and yet.
Darting about the eyes, very near. In the darling eye.

For Four Violins

Many were fascinated with birth in erratic modes of construal. Meaning?
If keen on jazz, why, I asked, did he borrow [the work of]
    Buxtehude. His name was Ben Paterson.
Ben, Fluxus.
From the start we witnessed birth and death shadow forth a heterodox
    enrollment to replenish the situation.

Measureless, sayable without toil, were Robert Gorham Davis's reappearing myths.
His students found places near their neighbors of last week.
By habit, the student preferred the company of one she met by accident once.
Inclusive of retrograde thematics, the manifestation of Davis.

Gather from time, and fourth generation variants, Buxtehude.
A natural situation sensibly represented in suitably receptive persons.
A natural vigilance sensibly represented.
Gather, from time and fourth generation variants, a phase
    elaborated with claim to plausibility.

In 1967, I heard a new release Ben wanted me to hear.
"What do you think?" he said. "Boring," I said. "Keep listening," he said.
"Now, what do you think?"
Steve Reich's new release, *Violin Phase,* interested Ben. He wanted me to hear it.

By habit we sat together.
A few notes rejuvenated when the new young god plays,
    when Paul Zukofsky's vigilant playing wore on.
Technique that elucidates process confers respect upon psycho-acoustic blur.
Common crystallizing devices such as the force of habit.

A minim of disenfranchisement.
"Boring," I said. "Keep listening," he said.
"What do you think?" he said. "Oceanic," I said.
A minim of anomie.

Drastic Measures

List names of persons.
With ski mask we approach the registrar.
Lacking imperative water, we staggered toward the registrar,
listing names of persons, dates of tenure.

Youth indicated
like a giant footprint;
the artist's imprimatur,
indicated. Such is youth.

An epistemological equivalent of hives or cystitis, indicating
    the ideological body is not well,
manages the volatile brew;
managing the brew, volatile and abundant
hives indicate our body.

You're impossible! All right, you're improbable.
An odor.
An odor rotating,
improbably you.

An odor shelved, or was it disallowed?
Stench in all singleness of heart,
a stench-filled room,
an odor of dereliction the library disallowed.

Whether malodorous people impinge
on others' rights
or the right of way
is an issue of free speech in some liberal resentment.

As we suffer a restaurant's good intentions,
odors, probabilities;
the new poets'
intentional restaurants.

At Princeton, the guys speak of restaurants
red,
feeling red—
the guys speaking of restaurants, the gals of intentionality,

as we did, as we might have done.
Feeling read
feeling read, an ontological claim said to inhere in the phenomenal
deeds we did, deeds we might have done.

Guitars and Tigers

Motionless against guy wires
across the loins in fixity,
to fix reference rather than to give meaning
or synonym for "guitar"

is "the length of S" designating the waxy
mentality plucked in leisure time;
time study: the study of work.
"The length of S" and "the length of S"

designating the same thing, waxing
this red. This red and that
wisp of red apprehension,
this in pursuant to directedness,

this business reply card.
"The length of S" designates a mention: Sloan-Kettering;
"The length of S" and "the length of S" and "the length of S,"
this, in exit

one meter long. Although a standard has no length,
the unmarked straightedge affixed there
refers now to a large Asian carnivore
having a tawny coat traversely striped with black.

Henry Cowell Plays the Standards

Science and Technology in Art Today
"These fragments I have shored . . ."

Modern American Usage
"From the steeples and mountains . . ."

To the Finland Station
The Poetics of Roman Ingarden

"I wandered lonely as a cloud . . ."
The Visionary Company

        □

The arachnid in art, these spinnerets from which . . .
these fragments I have shored . . .
these fractions converted to a failure,
these spinnerets from which issue silk

"filament, filament, filament"
from steeples to mountains far from being perturbed,
far from being perturbed more perfectly
in a litany of casting forth of

silk and number, or accolade:
"which consists in touching the recipient's cheek with one's own"
in touching the recipient with one's own usage,
Modern American Usage,

in which "acquiesce" meets "assent."
Auxiliary vines are strangling our factory;
a wall indecipherable within the stranglehold of vine.
Acquiesce, meaning "assent" or "submit."

To the Finland Station, a destiny.
Overgrown would suggest non-utility
of chimneys or of a sensitive child
This Way to the Waiting Room, go toward it but never attain

n-dimensional mentality. Throughout form-consciousness
strata come forth to upend curricula.
Nomenclature uncut. Strata come forth: Take courage!
In whatever alleged mentality, "valleys shall be raised up, and mountains made plain."

      □

These spinnerets from which issue failure drawn out
firm yet elastic, ductile
"till the ductile anchor hold"—
a finer technology in art, and he knew it.

The arachnid in art, these spinnerets from which . . .
These fragments I have shored . . .
these fractions converted to a failure,
these spinnerets from which issue steeples rotating

and minarets secreted from the abdomen
to enact the casting forth of effort,
to accelerate the casting forth of—
unfortunate minarets

bound in silk and number, not accolade:
"which consists in touching the recipient's cheek with one's own"
in touching the recipient with one's own usage,
Modern American Usage,

usage: "Acquiesce," meeting "dream"
on brick, ivy-laden,
ivy in ideological stranglehold,
meaning "assent" or "submit."

To the Finland Station.
Overgrown would suggest non-utility
of disused speech
after years affianced to exile. A figure, stationary

in disbelief. Overgrown would suggest non-utility
"simply by writing the word 'not.'"
If not, then not
in variegated stranglehold, overgrown light

and railway ties awash in creosote.
"As a cloud,"
as a cloud now overgrown,
as a cloud now overgrown the recipient's cheek.

THE WINDOWS FLEW OPEN

Respected, Feared, and Somehow Loved

In the long run we must fix our compass,
and implore our compass,
and arraign our shadow play in heaven, amid the pantheon
where all the plea-bargaining takes place.
                                        Within the proscenium arch,
the gods negotiate ceaselessly,
and the words he chooses to express the baleful phrase dare to be obsessed
with their instrumentality. Please send for our complete catalogue.

As in the days of creation, the clouds gossip and argue, the gods waver.
The gods oversee such unstable criteria as fourthly, fifthly.
The rest are little timbral touches.
The gods waver. To reiterate a point, the gods oversee
the symposium of the life raft—a crazed father, a dead son,
                                        an unwarranted curtailment of family.

Part of the foot, and thus part of the grace splinter in dismay,
and the small elite of vitrines where our body parts are stored
dies in a plane crash in Mongolia.
Why didn't someone do something to stop the sins of the climate,
                                        and earlier,

why did not someone rewrite the sins of the vitrines, the windows
shipwrecked icily, the windows called away?

Veil

An enchanted frame assures the image of a loved one.
Then there is the question of response.
A loved one produces things. Then there is this question
of existence.
                         Motion dashed to the ground,
and now a hapless pattern in its stead.
Little portions of liveliness are thrown out as inquiries.

Then there is the day that lives up to its preconceived ideas.
Then there is the day
empowered to train all sense on the moment,
holding onto that bias, often and later,
                                        although meanwhile,
the day is in position and has empowered the senses
to caress the starstruck flames,
the excited jets surrounding these inquiries.

                                   If there is a pattern
of stars beyond the starstruck blue, it spells desire,
and beyond this, a paler tendency
for stars to sift a desire to be anywhere, and you
not even among them in question form.

Publicly Silent

Events do not imply they are sealed off from each other:
you move so rapidly through awareness
and the self-awareness drizzling over it.

We hold onto each other, a bird and its beak,
but awareness brings us to the intersection
of perishable paper

and quietly strolls our eyes along the cut
as it makes of our bodies two
celestial phenomena: desire and knowledge

telling of many cuts in situ
until aware of our eyes in situ, although halved,
to draw our injury along the cut

and make of our one body, two,
and exact of our two repossessed bodies a rent
which falls from rock to rock to rock.

Within This Book, Called Marguerite

The sky is overcast and behind it an infinite regress
of vision is pulling nearer (and yet beneath)
in bashful ruts. I wonder if the mind will ever stop pursuing
rivals minds or at least rival murmuring. It is a long sky
that convenes this endlessness.

                                    Persons cunningly blent
to suggest a consensus—this is what is meant by serious entertainment
of opposing and hastening points of view, each of whose
sense of history is mutually exclusive.

                                    Deck chairs
are making a return. I remember when stacking and ganging
chairs were innovative and David Rowland won an industrial award
for the campanile of steel chairs climbing to the sky.

                                    As time separates us
from the evaporating architectonics to sweeten mythopoetic
substances, you start to count heroically,
hurled down upon a profile of an as yet
unrevealed know-how.

                                    You are unaccompanied
like the great unaccompanied counting
for solo violin that has arisen from the other side
of the mind and hand, the dark, tangled side of the hand,
with its great length of stay.

The Seasons Change

1.
It is very early.
She was not prepared to make the concessions her métier demanded.
The seasons change,
and with each season
it is the duty of fashion to render the body suppliant,
and to the woman living there
convince her she must spare
nothing: she must warp her anatomy as fashion says
for her own is wrong.

Every day and in every way
breath goes down in fire, long-waisted and vibrantly responsive,
while air carves up ars erotica.
It is the duty of fashion to reinvent fire, irony, stone, and air,
for anatomy is captive.

Improve the deep-set eyes of the Caribbean,
speak of a skull.
Into waiting vessels, into each ditch, a heart will follow.
You are flung aside
or played back and forth between the one and the many.
Lucky the reader who finds magnanimity
in the well-advertised physique of the Caribbean.

2.
Year by brittle year,
it is the duty of fashion to insist that anatomy is expendable
on one face, ethical on the reverse,
subject to the Hebraic-Christian estate
that may impute to good looks authenticity of being or wretchedness and folly.
Wonder of wonder: the field has eyes,
the fire pretends to be read by the kindling,
and fashion dictates the idiom solicitous of us line by line
while remaining unconvincing in each phase.
Crescent-shaped this season,
anatomy stays home wearing the casual shirt-dressing with details you'll love,
the assumption being that your very marrow is disloyal, forgetful material.

Shallow puddles freeze
and the morning finds them broken glass.

And speaking of "looks,"
the outward shape of the Thirties is calling you.
In matinee we have changed,
and to the simple inquiry, "Are you wearing silk?"
comes the unrehearsed, "No, I'm wearing a modern convenience,"
mimicking the synthetic
memoranda almost without knowing it,
impressionable even as each season "goes on loving after all hope is gone."

3.
To fashion, and thus to entertain
history strolls amid anecdote and light.
Even anecdotal matter finds imitating the zeal of the wind
light mental recreation. The chairs
of 18th-century France are set in amusing
configurations throughout the salon.
Throughout the salon,
the French say "amusing," meaning anything:

the tide of changing chairs improvising a tide
of couples and twos in light,
translucent and amusing tide pools.
This space, this infinite mobility
of a lightweight, altogether pierced, grove
of chairs is structurally commensurate
with everlasting gossip springing up
among an infinite supply of partners.

4.
"In thunder, lightning, or in rain,"
fashion charges anatomy to depart its condition, its space.
Why, in this atmosphere,
do we not blame the technologies of the sartorially ingenious?
This in hasty atmosphere.

The seasons went.
The lives in which we live become insolvent.

And they went down slowly, then fast.
Human and restless,
seasons never cease to amaze us for their versatility,

and for the full-scale illusionist realism
wherein we walk down city streets.
At their zenith
they seem all crossed out,
unanswerable and advancing, curiosity traversing the island.

Like shallow water,
our bodies learn to discard their extensive autobiography
once the prevailing attitude in clothing is disguised perniciousness
or wit: Mondrian in elevation,
Picasso in plan,

adding to the subject of oneself
fashion as co-author
and quick propagandist
ceaselessly emending the discernible silhouette
of the heroine's ten-year wanderings.

Carpet Within the Figure

1. Hercules as Inkstand

But notice, for example,
the past wants no less than to be a statuette
and to stay a little longer. All kinds of walking and seeing
are here to consider the stumbling block of this bronze.

Finally, a bit further on, where history may be,
and where viewing from all sides creates dance steps in exposition
of the thing, this Hercules, this bronze with its two tempestuous backs,
grapples with the wrestling people wish each other:

I dashed to the skillful place where *I had left it lying*
and under which—for the small silk wave was disarrayed—
runnels intend no less than wrestling
sedimented into artifacts;
then my stumbling, to my unutterable relief,
produced an answering untidiness:
I noticed some strife in *the windowblind,*
like victor and victim fused, *and then the child,*
swerving away, danced out, blushing and suddenly lamp-lit.

3. The Lute Player

Have you sent me this?
Have you sent for me?
Twisting the ends
belongs here.

Where is my gift?
Contemporaries report
her excavating in vain. . . .
Is this my gift?

Raising your hand, on request,
hoisting it high
in obedience, so to speak,
obedience hoisted

like a beacon
but a beacon
to be disbelieved;
and yet as one

who steps forward
and lividly survives
the space
corrugated with sounds

of singers singing,
so too the beacon
steps forward
and lividly survives

rusted steel
set on the road,
in obedience, so to speak,
to the repair

of the road
the repair
dragged
quite large

and rendered intelligible
on request.
Rusted steel,
we do not see steel today.

5. Carpet Within the Figure

Less like a sea, than a sea
that has stuck fast, exodus where repose is notorious and servants rush in
to obey the satrap's last command, who in carrying out his wishes bring innumerable
      torchlit belongings to coma.
And we can hurry our minds. And we are crying. And we are swept away by
flammable feelings of undetermined origin,
the way a river refers to the many relatives of the disappeared and consumed.

The way a river refers to the many sites of oblivion, some reclining,
some instrumental in bringing confusion to storm. In a canopied place
"too far from the stars,"
where repose is notorious and half-spoken to himself,
less like a sea, than a sea that has stuck to itself in extreme passivity
or extreme position, the extremity of the self enacted through the body—
these peaches, pears, grapes, trailing harnesses
never to be defined beyond the impermanence of a handful,
unerring to him for the last time.
And we can hurry our minds.
And we are swept away by flammable enthusiasms.

Buried as we were under the weight
of political resolve, and strapped to the earth
as if the earth were alive and we ourselves
were inside it, we emit a scent
and a language enmeshed in human affairs.
A leg dimly suggesting a cast of a leg,
and a chair inverted, for him with legs,
are very explicit pressures, reachable, thinkable.

A leg, bent and dimly suggesting the cast of the cast
of the earth, is, at any rate, strapped to a language
buried under the weight of human affairs.
Inside we emit a shred, and we ourselves
then become thinkable by a ship
slitting the water with its prow
and writing on our minds as if the earth were alive
and we ourselves were inside it.

Rich still lifes suggesting a cast of a leg,
for him as for others, are thinkable in a love-hate absorption
with things and with things made contingent.
A cast of a leg in retrograde suggests a crisis lengthwise.
Neither coin nor gem,
the disappeared were less decent than a river, a river aroused.

Pushing a massive pyre into the past, we are reachable by melodrama
as if the earth were alive, but taking an extreme position within the symbol.
Less like a sea, than a sea
in extreme passivity or extreme position, the extremity of
exodus enacted through the flesh,

where repose in notorious and servants rush in
to obey the satrap's last command like a sea carrying out wishes, carrying in
the tributaries of the disappeared,
he is so much smaller than the ignorance which had been everything.

Wild Sleeve

Falling from a sleeve,

the meanders in Figure One, and wildness
anterior to pattern
in lines that swim with every response.
The audience finds them beautiful.

"White lines meander wildly over a black ground,"
the question is . . . and a hand
churns across the vulnerability at home.

White lines swimming away . . . ,
but then isn't that dismissing them too early?
How erasures crush and how a shadow leaves for what is not
even a dawn. What is holding this drama together?
The least swimming casts notions prophetically into ordinariness
though ordinariness seems least possible.

White, wild emergencies want our path, or rather the entire sky
folds in the hand like a trick. Neither you nor I
admire the maneuver drawn from the sleeve
of the guileless: "Wings of swans that wounded us"
because they were beautiful and because they were a trick.

And here are emergencies that streak
across a dark sheet of paper, quick and inventive, anatomically correct:
Isn't that too early?
The summer is crushing and impossible.
It is impossible to draw these innumerable responses, the white flowers
that trick and suffocate us. Drowning in flowers,
we leave fascination to the fascinated.
"Because of their beauty they wound us."

In the history of pattern, antecedent wallpaper
is murderous, quick, and only later, a bower welcoming sedated peonies
which sends the possibility of a perfect
abridgment of wildness; and so we leave. A belated thank you
for inviting us to your home.

                    In Figure Two
an abetting landscape of a mind's voluntary betrayal
of its own xenophobia shows itself
when the host adopts the manners and customs of the stranger
who is his guest. The exit surrounding his mind
unfolds symmetrically planted apology and lupine,
growing among the verticals that float the hand.

Blood or Color

Across a room,
a handshake in a late, large design
has caught the overflow of the heart, the human figure as a source.
"Have you sent me my bouquet of gladiolus?" the poet asks.
"No, I haven't," I say, "but I have emphasized it."

Across a room, a writer queries,
"Have you reached my claim check and my watercolors,
    have you introduced a bouquet of gladiolus?"
"No," I say, compressed in ambiguous space,
"but I have brought you your bouquet of gladiators."

"No," I say,
"but as in the arena of this room,
interrogation is impaled on intimacy: gladiators burst
and metamorphose into the womanly bright remains of our city."

This pediment forfeits nothing; these gladiators are inextinguishable.
The most brilliant blue eyes obtained by natural means
flare as if in a greeting, herd, or flock.
A herd or flock is numerically great.
Is this my gift: the human figure pierced and confessed?
But the sky had altered:

Pierced and splashed, and driven
like the arena of command
drives the volume, line, and light
of rooms we enter,

here is a man, some victory;
some victory, though not all of it,
some victory with outstretched arm
like Alexander,

the marble face
with hurtful tools at the deepest level.
"They are afraid of you.
That's why they are so obsequious."

Some Street Cries

1.

Trees, good new trees, trees that are stitched
into tinware by the sun.

Tanned arms sweep around a pin;
the tanned arms of someone grow and wane.

This roof takes three times as long as leather
to deliberate, to settle over the houses,

but hospitality takes three times longer,
longer than the thong of leather I had made for you.

A walnut is of two minds, touch and go.
Here, the gong of street cries scouring the street:

will you hear it,
will you wear it?

Will you wear this gaping mask? With childlike arms?
Will you buy this broom, this candle with its mask?

These powerful arms that sweep? The arms that grow
like a tan, or the arms that grow and tan

and wane into a variant of leisure?
What work do you have?

2.

If he says, "I have it but will not give it to you,"
that is theft. The law knows it is negative
to refrain from doing that which he should do

and fail to do that which he should do.
That is theft, and he is a serpent.
In the almost launched quiet he will not give it to you,

for he is withholding your salary. To you
I say, "That is theft, he is a cheat
who refrains from doing that which he should do

and is proud of it." It is up to you
to call him on it, to call him a rat,
and if he says, "I have it but will not give it to you,"

or if he says, "I owe it but will not pay you"—
this last a denial less stiff-necked than the rest
of his story, but still a refrain about doing and failing to do

that which is proper—remind him: you
both know he is in violation of five negative
commandments and one positive commandment—that is, if
he hang fire—knowingly undoing that which he should do.

3.
He swallowed handfuls of peanuts, which were very salty.
Try these peanuts, these precious shouts
hawking odd angles, flung sideways.
Hawking odd bodies flung sidearm, pleasure in quantity
through pleasure not entirely pleasurable.

As with dogs whose deep-set heart is confiscated, flung
with shouts of reprimand,
he chewed half-measures of salty peanuts
and sought a finger-width of pleasure from the city stoop.
He sought shouting, then the confiscated
shouting unable to silence handfuls of running.
He swallowed handfuls of peanuts, as when dogs run against the grain
of shouting and snapping of fingers; as dogs run themselves senseless,
so, too, the heart and throat drive on.

Try these peanuts, these peanuts however salty,
these peanuts, even as swallowing famishes itself
in pleasure not entirely pleasurable.
Take up peanuts for pleasure
and swallowing that gives pleasure however adversive.
No one denies it. "Thus he could charm."

How can we console ourselves
if the pleasures on which we rely for comfort
refresh pleasure with pain. As dogs run,
we seek unexpected angles of frustration
in snouts, eyes, and tongues. Taste these smarting sensations
flung to the yelping dogs, and try pleasure
heavily ruffled by the panting, circling
animals alive by your hand.
As dogs run, so pleasure salty grain by salty grain.
Crescents, hexagons of salty peanuts, delectable and corrosive,
are swallowed riotously for days.

4.
I think I shall end by not feeling lonesome,
only scoured by the lengthy light of everyone.
Nice, fine milk, the best of all milk.

Balancing the persuasive long pole
of friendship on a stone,
I think I shall end by not feeling lonesome.

I have lived and eaten simply.
I have leaned against the shape of handsome choices.
This almanac conceals a pasture you would like.

The universe is cast in consequences.
Draw my name in milk on canvas.
I doubt I shall and by not feeling lonesome,

but this is outrageous:
come buy my ground ivy, come buy my water cresses.
The ink is wrong, but a battered almanac is not a heartless almanac.

But is it time to combine and speak out?
The day gazes helplessly at time.
I think I shall end by not feeling lonesome,
the pamphlets yellow, the milk also: the milk, the fine milk.

5.

Give a sphere new life
by ruling it with lines of evergreen.
I promise you ink that branches and conceives!
I promise you all of utility!
I promise you black freshets and gray,
a few drops are all you need, ladies!

Like news in a newsreel,
you hold your forbidden body high at a tiring angle.
And then, o stratosphere, you hold a spark to mathematics:
the universe is alive very fast, the idea showers down
alive with proof, although the proof itself
takes so long to resemble its intuition.
When you sing you sing at the top of your lungs.

How these obliterating things are made!—wonder is instantaneous,
but the "sometimes harsh facts" of wonder intertwist.
The idea is how to wrap five eggs,
the promise to work it through accomplished in steel.
Throughout heaven and earth, the cry for help prospers,
accomplished in sisal within earshot of work.
Until you touch bottom, the cooper's struggle takes a while.

Give a sphere new life
by ruling it with evergreen.
I promise you a plan
and a path without pain!

6.

Insects are good creatures, bells dazzle.
Flying insects paste themselves to streetlights.
Splash knives on marble. Ashes, ashes for example.

Splash knives on marble to obtain a reply
from the ladies and gentlemen interwoven.
Paste chutes under ladders, paste napkins to bells.

Won't you buy a few sprigs of rosemary
from ladies interwoven like self-abolishing lace?
Splash knives on marble: ashes, ashes for example.

Ladders leap to the chimney,
spread the word. Insects fly fast through spaces
arranged by ladders; bells dazzle.

I wish you a child pulling a pull-toy
and all increase. All increased
like knives on marble. Shove, stab, and fall

across the human family
who has commenced to extinguish itself.
Paste chutes to ladders, paste napkins to bells,
splash knives on marble: ashes, ashes, for example.

Still to Come

The hotel is preoccupied with our dangling,
fragilely physical
gaze. Once thought to have been destroyed

even the possibility we are lost
is utilized. As if animated by foot pedals, exits open
and close and bring anonymous philanthropy to the page

appreciating here.

                    Once thought to have been destroyed,
even the possibility we are lost
seems coiled flesh and blood: blood of blue light

carrying through to their objects
and lying in the round, coherent space
"now laid solitary in his sleep."

The Diaries Began

Whatever he might mean by "dark Satanic mills,"
afflicted like so many subjects, the entrapment being gossip
spinning among her maids, spinning hair.

We are now in the middle of a similar bulk,
as birds sway across this violet planet
and banter with this cardboard. We live the way we do.

The diaries began so that the inconceivable might be said
with no hint or substitute: curdling hair, shrieking.
We are now near the middle of a similar bulk

of avid history. Birds sway,
rashes migrate across the surface of our inner workings.
The diaries were begun, and ideology had its audition
with no hint or substitute, but with spinning hair spinning to the floor.

A Way of Life

The vintner says, "There is no prohibition against putting off a tourist needlessly."

As a tourist aches, as a tourist experiences the entailment
of Europe without words and only a wallet to express,
feeling adult but stored within the body of an infant,

you may bathe now
on the stairs
of voices.

And so when the concierge says that a tourist is one
who does not speak, who does not dream, and who is not born
presupposing our language, we cannot say there has been a violation
if the tourist among us catches the historical entailment.
The concierge does not touch his arm, however,
to remind him of the predatory numbness setting in
and what will follow: feeling foreign from morning to noon.

Even a vintner catches the entailment of Europe.
You may bathe now on the stairs of voices,
but the concierge will balk at linking arms with you.

Skin

Our skin: strenuously tutored to appreciate the vernacular
body a feeling might have. Companies
of hands, legs, cigarettes, a whip, the sea
tangle in the mutilated lamplight,

and wrap an intelligent enterprise in a gang of approaches.
I think that black into pink is devastating. A bitter winter,
the whip, the sea—all familiar rubble that comes around nightly,
but so familiar, the feeling need only mention surrender and we surrender.

In the postwar victory, lamplight is harsher, categorical.
Pink is devastating, a stone lawn.
A great part of the American pavilion
has been given over to an iron blue and magnificent écorché—

the spirit, when the spirit is flayed and forbidden
to talk about itself. It feels normal
to live in the present amid musculature
of beautiful early work propped against an uphill sea.

Crossing Disappearing Behind Them

Diverse strangers flower and diverge,
and when they cross paths, three strangers flower
and are clairvoyant. Under the moon, combining voyages,
it is their turn to appear whole in silhouette.
The street expresses it,
and it is all you can do to keep the shrill silhouette
where this occurred, which in retrospect
seems the intrigue of passing and coalescing.

Crisscrossing within the otherwise vague
whereabouts helping them, strangers
stray into circumstantial flare, bright and shapely
in disproportion to the event.
The street expresses it as if speaking in words,
and when they cross, strangers comply with passing
and coalescing and flowering.
Their pretty accident goes behind,
their coalescence disappears, and then speaking disappears
into the dismemberment of coalescing and passing human effect.

Someone throws a vista across a tree, and you, too,
are alive. It is raining pliable flowers.
Three in slangy attire cross under a tree
and disappear, crossing disappearing behind them.
It is raining, but this is common practice.
In keeping with this, a minor shadow
occurs by passing by, throwing its half-truth forward,
being original only less excellent
than untruth his shadow has produced. This application is lengthy
and comes with two interleaved carbons.

The sky issues rain.
The sky issues rain hesitantly,
but then the sky seems necessary.
Issuing massive rain,
lifelike petals begin to fail,
and paper bends away.

Petals bend shadow, being minor
in a minor station, though no less original.
An original turn performed less well
than the turn that bears his name, and you,
promptly this, wearing a vinyl raincoat,
push open the plate glass doors to be spared
being called minor for wearing the same
rechargeable and independently arrived at footprint.

Being minor means that an era haunts a phrase of ruined memorabilia,
floral commemorative move across you.
A quoted feeling hangs over the ruin, the vinyl, the rain,
each in its landscape. The vinyl, the ruin, each
has memorized the original one in each of us
who wears a paraphrasable vastness
in virtue of arriving late.

And on the fortieth day
after I wrote that the poem you called derivative
is original if late, I opened the door
and the windows flew open
in a revolutionary manner, bare-breasted
and I saw myself
stepping onto a movie set of rain imitating rain,
a central fiction.

The ruin has memorized the ruin, and so, too, the vinyl
in each one of us replicates the original vinyl
of some unsuspecting excellence.
He who is truly original did not intend this dusk.
At first glance, this is dusk led into a past
where rain pours down an original thought
springing from as many heads.

Floral commemoratives
and the arrested growth of the silhouette of one thought
are flung across several minds
and out onto the real floor of the night.
You are wearing vinyl, she is wearing it,
and their silhouette creates more of the same copious thing
not far away, so we remember this corridor forever.

A Full Hand

1.

As when the plan to escape has gone astray,
or as when plans have slipped from the table
and the fallen portion has knelt
on one knee, deferring to the slanting roof, or cornice,
and the consequential slant of postponement from within
continually defers to deep disappointment.
And you, what will happen to you?
And it is just this falling that will have happened
and will happen, continually embarrassing every hour,
bowing low; bent as prescribed, this feeling for numbers
will continue to sequence the cornice
in which the dying warrior assumes the dying-warrior pose.

Neither standing nor sleeping, the plan to leave
slipping, with postponement so assumed
I cannot imagine myself free-standing, only occasioned
and partial in both children lying down
like pillars attached to procrastination.
Still, I hereby affirm
the pen is on the table, the draft is pure surface,
and only when the plan to leave my thoughts and actions
to your looming thought has been postponed,
do the fallen threaten
to end there and then, within the hour
no longer allowable.

It is just this,
it is the following: on hurtling the spear into clouds.
Sighing is not known by these people.
Sighing, hurtling as far as it will travel.
And it is the following: they do not know how to sigh;
they withdraw but they do not sigh.
Add to this that which will happen
on hurtling spears when sighing is not admissible.
They do not sigh, although they hurtle their spear
and lead and smother distance. And it is merely this:

when they are sad, they surround their sadness
and hurtle it as far as it will go
and return to society empty.

2.

What is the intent of these lost causes,
as when postponement
puts miles between us and the congealed
foothills hanging fire

and retreats rank and file into the lesson
in which we are sequestered?
Is it simply this clear of striding
existence in polychromy

that is handsome, with all striding
divided by tenths, one degree for each mortal country
on consignment to us? This soldier is handsome
because he excels at mortality.

And it is just this clear division of striding
by degrees, starting from the vertical
and winding down through what one knows
forewarned by the pediment.

What one knows is calibrated dying, starting from
standing, moving through the ephemeral
metropolitan fighting
to arrive, at last, at horizontal rhetoric

carefully rotated so we can learn from it.
By this reasoning, striding is preliminary,
laughing has its explosive,
sleep is delicately borne upon the shoulders of medics,

every way of being meted out on the ruler
of being, and even dying enjoys a measure
between spur and spurn, loaf and lord,
although it is exactly this declension that carries us off.

Writing to have happened, while living within the silent day
like two desirable things that desire each other,
I desire this day. Today seems a divested possibility.
A similar drift of postponement

remains central to ourselves,
and the weaponry (as you have guessed)
presses forward, like one desirable thing.
Just this arsenal of distance

delivered today with an expedient thrust
to the stomach, sharp down to the depth
of his belly, unharnessed him
for eternal dénouement.

3.
The postponement is hurtled at night,
dangled before every shining day,
traveling through and through. You in your blouse,
you in unwilling armor, and you as you are.

You in your open air
are the mixture
that hurtles at night
and catches it under the chin strap.

When not transparent
hurtling through, skillfully,
and breathing again
when not battling the night, dismantling it,

the wind wears its blouse. You are normal,
with moist lips,
far-striking and harvested
in the gymnasium of the night garden.

Delete "gymnasium." Delete "night garden."
In the delicate gymnasium of battle they knelt, as between rooms,
while the consequential warrior combed the night and the night became him.
This was his strength, his taste for continual forward motion,

fairly shaped by other theatrics,
but fairly etched with the premonition that appointed him
to render the rest of us harmless.
In the delicate gymnasium of metal against metal,
the new historians have been struggling; and you,
what will happen to you, you are deleted,
you who are vanished? The hour was not presented,
but stippled with the premonition of response, always just inches away.

"Like clouds before dawn,"
the question is why the door seduced the characters around it,
and the female reader especially, into an impressive array of waiting.
Laughing nervously, caught about the waist, the appointment fell delicate, dead-pale.
Certainly the shape on which dust has focused is expecting us.
We, certainly, are expecting our share of the spoils.
But dawn does not bring to accomplishment all thoughts in men's minds,
the prix fixe of picture and dream;
rather, mounted upon a convenient viewing stand,
the problem is expecting us to be supple, easily surrendering.
And so the gate was made to open. Sky-filling,
calling aloud, the spear met its blouse, slid through
the causeways of the sleeping blouse mother was wearing
and her limbs lost their strength. They left these to lie there,
with strength streaming from her translucent eyes:
are you falling back my brave horses?—
and as they left these to lie, advance turned into retreat,
and delirium was not difficult. Strangers led the children away.
In and out and up and down, let us remember
a redeeming feature sliding over a countenance is sad.
As when plans fall aslant and a spear lands
nowhere in particular, yet unabashedly personal
and chaste in its own way, our appointment was pretty;
unguents, too, passed through her blouse without difficulty.
Our appointment went delicate, like a leaf, or like a redeeming feature
mouldering, incapable; and in its place, the cancellation
of this pretty appointment sank.

TWO POEMS

Setting, or Farewell

1.

What is amazing about this clapping
is that it is effortless,
as effortless as silver in a mirror collecting gazes.
Given someone striding through an exit,
marauding, conclusive—a silver bracelet
with light "dancing," as they say—
the idyll might be reconstructed.
But then the answer is empty,
so human and ceaselessly
without recognition of anything.
It is effortless, without recognition
of anything passing between them.
It is effortless to pass between them,
excusing ourselves.

                 Then it is intermission.
It is noon, with provision
to forget all that came before and will come after.
We laugh because it is easier
to do than not to do,
to dismantle that demanding recital
blown from a molten, traveling drop of glass.

An averted gaze is like the shadow of a doubt.
"What are you practicing?"
"The next two days."
"Don't let them make *you* crazy,
you make *them* crazy."

2.

Being so empty, our hands sail into nothing.
We are incapable of anything,
let alone taking a bite out of the horizon,
but here we are in this place.
I remember crossing the prosaic sea,
never seeing the sun, going forth
as if it were a privilege.

                    I dream of night.
First nothing, then a fleet of ships
inflated with luck, then night.
Then night, then a fold,
then another strand of time or floating phrase
trusted to chance. This gold chain, for instance,
opportunely drifting toward us,
spoons and fibulae,
also coins that effortlessly detach themselves
from wants and desires
by way of the practical solutions they bring.

This gold chain, for instance,
these slivers shimmering around the throat of a loved one,
these phrases passed back and forth
found in the hoard of Scythian housewares
amass a style of being dead.
And you may submerge a time of hazardous speculation
the epoch only confirms.
As we sit on cushions, another strand of conversation
reaches over, in a room where not even anxiety
will deter the lithesome receptions.
Another nomadic phrase from another time drafts into this time,
without regard. The decor is opportune, if hazy.
Clouding the carpet are several hazy cushions for gesturing,
"This gold chain, for instance . . . ,"
ankles spanning the cushions like filament,
little silver rivers seen from airplanes.

Ships with feathered hulls
and effortless gold chain with its heavy, heavy links
seem alive; what do you think—are they alive for you?
A keel of snow rises from every ledge,
how is this example alive?
How does it compare with our gentle seasonal affection
for beautiful white shapes?
Light falling across the night snow as across a helmet,
with all that time before and after,
defines our stranded existence.
How is this an example?

How much does this gold chain cost to send
from coast to coast,
to New York? Perhaps the thing
that most impresses us is what refutes our lives
as we would like them to be: the safety pin
impaled on walls and floors of the exhibition.
Impressive is its escarpment
of knowledge, majestic long after the pin itself
is extinguished. And so little left to break.
What remains of the Scythians is a notion
that the safety pin is consequential technology
in pursuit of love
despite the brute,
non-visual aspect of the rest of it all.

3.

The curvilinear is operative; are you alive for it?
The ardent, starry grasp, seasoned with doing
and doing for its own sake, is operative too.
The forge is alive,
the proceeds of which go to benefit this harsh life.
First nothing, then
a fleet of ships like an emerging city
breaks the horizon, proving for once and for all
its punctual arrival. Then this ore happens.
The silver clasps are ready,
the duck-headed snakes, effortlessly golden
biting their own high-spirited tails.

It is unrecognizable so as to be unrecognizable
as human skin.
Anyway, I don't know what you are talking about.
For once and for all, they arrive on our amazed doorstep,
and this makes history.
Skilled at going forth, they also grasp
the tactical niceties of jewelry design.
First nothing, then a fleet of ships,
doing for the sake of doing, feathers the oar.

There is night in the balcony surrounding the lake.
This is a memoir,
and like the tree among trees that does not belong,
context declines something smooth and symmetrical.

There is night in the mirror surrounding the lake.
This is a mirror you say.

HANDWRITTEN

Among Them All

A car turning onto a driveway. An activity
that slows down activity. Also a routine
associated with domestic life, heard from inside.

The front tires passing through a puddle and dully
hitting a curb, then the rear tires
passing through the same, rolling onto the same
soothing routine, make me think that after rain
each dip is an excuse to change timbre.
The wet, the partially wet sounds of paint rollers
pushed from the gutter of a tray are the tires also.
I remember now I heard the car approach,

its description
ushered softly forward, growing louder, turning.

Fête Champêtre

1.
Remembering each careful window
and remembering how each braced the clean
indebted farmhouse, I am surprised by the casual way
the same windows are leaving the yard
and environs uninterpreted.
Around the house the birches bear vague and soft attitudes.
We have been approached by them
and the contents of our village have been spilled onto
the floor without hesitation.

The hopeful were buoyant,
it is fair to say prevalent, as the meteorite
is serenely contemporary in the sky.

I hear a branch
of a tree remembering the other short branches
as it falls accidentally.
Blue jays fly in, mounting the easygoing immersion
that continues outside,
weaving back and forth over it.
Double its length and increase the number
of birds flying in and out
"Actors and actresses created a role
which deepened and enriched the impression,"
and this awards my eyes a scrim
through which the sumptuous begins its climb.

I admired the restored torso,
as, for example, when one's enemy is admired without bitterness.

2.
Light thrown on stone
spotted with lichen shows how
a deer seen in early morning retains the word "deer."

And the provenance of silver maple,
butternut, spruce, pine, and birch
is not disturbed. It might be interesting to explore

attitudes curators have toward the exemplary
if mutable ideal,
plastic segued to marble
where the original parts are missing or splattered,
in order to restore
the pectorals to their original dazzling eloquence,
with another piece of plastic
tenderly leading the flank to its groin. And spotlighting

conceives of still another body within the original.

I hear a branch
of a tree hitting the other short
branches as it encounters falling,
a bagatelle in a forest of falling sounds.
I imagine you have come up behind me,

although the original impulse awoke
in a farmhouse years ago thinking, "Either the windows are immune
to scenery, or they have taken pleasure in being inclusive,

passive, almost uncomplaining."

Picture Collection

IMMIGRATION, WOMEN IN INDUSTRY, AGED,
COSTUME—1870S—AMERICAN,
MUSIC, TITLE PAGES—MUSIC,
UNEMPLOYMENT, CROWDS, SPECTATORS,
NEBRASKA—1899 AND EARLIER,
NEBRASKA—INDUSTRIES, IRON AND STEEL INDUSTRY,
COLLEGIATE LIFE—1970S.

The troop trains. It could be the jitterbug the way the soldier
hoists the girl to his window to kiss her, two guys
doing the boosting. But in most photos
the man and the woman are in a smash up,
and on the platform, out of their territory, a buddy
stands inside his duffel body.

Each folder is like the miscellany on your desk,
disrespectful when you search
for some one thing. Here is an engraving,
titled *Entrée du Duc d'Alençon,* 1582.
But you are not looking for this.

ARRIVALS AND DEPARTURES—some categories
hurt more than others,

the truly painful not being
the SUICIDE, but the folder when she comes back,
all of them sitting around the table
telling her how to behave.

Here is an engraving
titled, *Entrée du Duc d'Alençon,* 1582,
but you do not have the strength
for this nor for
the envelope of the man at the desk
intercepted by other business,
never quite absorbed in you.

Even so you notice everything.
As if it were spring the duke is received
by budding cannon. All along the wall
deciduous clouds,
and today, for him, the heavy municipal buckle is open.
Sheaves of spectators are watching the long suite
on horse and on foot, carrying lances,
carrying crossbows, seeing it lead
and finesse the climactic horse.

Escapade

I want you to accept a gallery that is also a tunnel
yet I disguise it, saying something nonchalant.
Nevertheless, I bring you two together.
There are no partitions and the owners sit way back
on a bench, resembling Moore's very stable
King and Queen.

The exhibit is inconsequential, but we move
trying to taper off gradually
because I once reviewed a show of theirs
and because turning back is like respecting
the considerable deck between us.

I think of them again. They have become an alloy
of bronze, monarchy, and shells.
Moreover, it is you who rally them
saying, "Why don't you put paintings along the staircase?"

But the accountant is still totaling
your exact words, and now it is,
"Why don't you hang paintings on the staircase—
of this artist, so-and-so, and Hans Werner Henze."

Dreams use our half-knowledge to advantage.
Nomenclature we hardly have a feeling for,
famous people who are peregrine
and live in planes, and whose career has a wingspan,
yet even those who are just names to us
can deposit the whole meaning.

I wonder what it would be like if sculpture were stolen.
The door opens, a proxy comes in
and steals a sculpture,
but instead of the usual tasteless exposé
the dream goes downstairs to the luncheonette
and orders steak.

He had brought his carbon-steel steak set,
yet inexplicably the steak is now London broil.
Even the dull end of a scalpel
can tease the bundled roast, and he does, carefully
slicing off the suffix
and the prefix, and leaving the interior, most red
syllable, the disclosed "rose" or "love."

An Emptiness Distributed

Without people,
a train station, an auditorium
seems visionary. The lower level
smells of insulation, and wind
from a still lower level, but no one is applying it.
You can feel the paths blowing through pores,
evaporating.

A slow torrent
falling headlong like escalators, or
perhaps streams run by electricity.
Have you ever seen escalators from the side?
Only the handrails move.

Levels,
each with its own set of handrails,
where the farther level is
not necessarily the deeper.

Someone is coming up
wearing a cap. Looking where his is facing
he would be the man striking
the match in the small room on stage.
Acting is more candid seen from the side
because it is pitched to someone else.
Another man is coming up
on another escalator. A few people
are stepping onto a Down escalator, a dance consisting of—
there could be a dance
consisting of bunches of people stepping
onto and riding banks of escalators
into fresh water, and having pushed off,
becoming slowly sedate.

Bordering on Skill

A few soap bubbles
met us as we climbed tiredly out
of the subway, and by the time we realized
they were indeed soap bubbles,
they had disappeared into the coats.
That boy leaning over a sill
like a carpenter's son is making them.
The sill is a frame in its least assuming form,
everywhere present,
underscoring the meaning of someone,
yet unseen, or seen as one of many
thresholds that are always occurring.
But aside from its emphatic function,
it is for shoring up intimate objects like arms
and breath concentrated on the adventure.

Muted pleasures like arriving home,
introduced into art as the aptitude of the middle class,
or as one artist told me "Once it belongs to artists,
it becomes everyone's"—Liberty Leading the People.
Arriving home we are free to reject this
coercion. We push everything back
and enter a place that in a different sense is settled,
rooms whose contents have settled.
Furniture rests on its low legs,
sometimes delineated but usually vague,
furniture and space made of the same substance,
day in and day out.
Coordination happens
when measuring water or finding the level for our arms.

Pulling ourselves from the imperviousness
into which we had descended, we saw some bubbles
and the sullen stairs through them before they burst.
This immediately changed my attitude:
the wavering boundaries became firm
and I walked across.

The vicissitudes floated down;
and that directed boy,
leaning out of the window and blowing bubbles,
came into mind later as another possibility.

Offering

A large concrete room standing idle,
stripped to the walls

like Arcadian bathers, or boys
posing as Arcadian bathers?
is the place whose entire light
and space is the sculpture.

And twenty years earlier the flow of activity
at the waterfront was made into a movie.

The pastoral lunch break set among buildings
is still another of these temperate experiences
that brings life before your eyes as a unit.

"Trembling saline light," he said,
meaning the quality of experience one has
standing in the empty clocktower
of a former insurance building.

Considerable Leisure

Stepping into the temperatures of the stream,
I felt the bed,
the intricate temperatures
quickening and in some sense giving rise to the slate bed,
which I doubt would have been as hospitable
with as many resting places if the water had not made the rock
passable, a concourse that let us walk easily:
in fact, there were a few of us walking downstream.
I guess what excited me most was
the license to enter and merely be there,
and then I enjoyed letting it go on and on like tap water,
the permissive current letting me stretch out
or arrange the bed so that several temperatures
passed through my body at once.

Something as unapproachable as maturity
put in layman's terms yet not scaled down
or vitiated is what I believe I became part of
when I entered the stream. And it was the same
as I had imagined by looking. And for a while
I enjoyed the fast, ingratiating current
and the slate, which was becoming passive
with many resting places and companions.

Like a figure whose awkward weight you see entering
a courtyard, closer to the activity than it has ever been,
I stepped into the stream
and onto the clarified plan.
What I enjoyed most was being able to enter
the thoroughfare and arrive
into the present for sure as another object
sheared by fast moving warm water.

Careers

How long we sit in front of them.
Compared with experience, this is gentle.
As if we are going on a long, persistent cruise
to be worn down.

My nephew thinks a fireman is a person
who starts fires. Wonderful.
Then a waterman is someone putting them out.
One composition goes like this:
"The fireman is someone who starts the barbeque.
Arriving with his lighter fluid,
he is cheered by everyone, including mothers and fathers.
Then his face grows serious.
He goes over and ignites the grill."

The hardwood in the fireplace is insurmountable.
The first blaze of newspaper shrivels.
We begin again, using spurs and branches
to trap the fire, and then we try a jack
and a stirrup made from our hands,
filling a blue book with wild guesses.
Meanwhile someone comes forward to study the principle.

"It was not, of course, human."
The fireplace, like a "low, pinched braincase"
stared into the room, a container with no memory
of body heat and no feeling for it.
When building a house people embedded a skull in its center;
for centuries they warmed themselves by this contradiction.
With even points like a violin phrase repeated
and ignited over and over for a half hour,
each attack vigilant—the combustion
is what makes the piece, while the most uneven theme
is our attention, which tends to back away,
succumbing to middle distance, asking what else there is,
yet returning. Looking into it, even looking for it.

Toying with pastimes, and in relation to them, our masterful size.
The adult games self-contained
in a plastic cube are attractive.
The wave, for instance, a section of which
in a case, tilts, the blue-tinted water
crashing one side, then leveling off
before piling and mechanically crashing the other.
The section of anything is interesting.
Another everyone has seen is the shallow oval of sand,
two different weights, two different colors.
The smokiest possible heap
does not deter gravity from sorting it all.
Tableaux from which we draw morals,
the diminution that transforms the ignored
natural occurrence into an object,
thereby a goal. The fire in the fireplace
and the others of the pantheon, the earthquake,
the tidal wave, should in turn while we sit around
play in a recessed place in the walls of our homes.

Sometime during his youth or during the course of an evening
someone shows an aptitude for it and is allowed to preside,
and it becomes his phenomenon. He literally stirs the wind,
the warmed water swelling into a canopy of water,
sending uncatalogued feelings in advance. When a storm develops
on its own, he sits down. "The torrential rains begin."
Stones and rocks strategically gathered
into bulwarks withstand the slicing
rains for quite a while before giving up.
The point is to build something
not so that it lasts forever but that it dies
in the most developed way possible.
That is why he gets up and uses the bellows
to fuel the wind.

Beyond the smiling seated man, in a sense within
the property left over from his L-shaped pose, there is a fire
"raging" throughout a house, and a company—No. 7—
pulling a hose toward it.

Fugio

fugio (fyŌŌ′ jē ō) n. A copper coin, the first
U.S. coinage authorized by Congress, 1787,
bearing the word *fugio* beside a meridian sun
and the motto Mind Your Business. [L., I flee]

Visiting a friend starting in business
presses the exact center of appropriate feelings.
We bring flowers. Enterprise is freshly seen;
we like to think it lifts by our being there,
standing around, making the store plump. But it is the owner
who enables our carnations and allows us
to choose the vase. We set an amenable doily
between the glass and the mahogany, feeling flushed.

Striped carnations are dogmatically festive.
What do they stand for—a kind of pluck?—
or pluck verging on self-interest, and the whole corner
looking like July 4th
on Elm Street, when flags were flown in the centers of lawns?
The breezy stores, the scores of sheet music
celebrating Admiral Dewey, our own glamour.
Many plastic Bicentennial flags are more patriotic.
A beauty shop's red, white, and blue
plastic carnations show no cunning, in the window,
the three or six of them spread far apart to look full.

The memorial is surrounded
with tissue-protected illustrations by John Sloan.
The Sloans do not give much: the convention of going downstairs
in the dark, with the darkness
that astonishes a small identity midstep,
an atmosphere introduced, a soft imperative
regarding this flower.
That it takes a moment from our lives
somehow makes it plausible.

Fading motives that revive when we look at them dug up,
sitting in their clump of earth.
Sometimes it is enough to compile them,
bringing their different sources together,
to feel forgiven and calm.

Smooth and Rough

Convention favors the right hand
and always attaining the top and bottom line (the stems
rising farther than this), and that the main roads
have cursive intersections like script.
Placed above the blackboard
the row of cards was a model blackboard.
I remember thumbtacks sinking through,
and when I looked at the letters
I liked the warmth of "a" near "A," "b" near "B,"
daughter near mother, but I did not believe
in consistently smooth features;
the handsome model is not credible, in movies
handsome lines should be said by ugly men.

Inquire Here

The door cautions you about something
rehearsed in these studios, yes very much
like a thought that shadows you. You

are the window for all prompt magic:
a speeding train, or perhaps your good health. Like a bus
that throws a shadow over you

as it passes, ordinary caution
arrives. Your health is beyond influence—
but your appearance! The curtain arrives as you.

The traveling theater will be your well-being.
You are the window for all that sullen reference.
(When the bus arrives) with your window,

you will disappear. Good luck! Something
indelible: the bus arrives like a bus.
Your face is polished, sloping as you

hold your ticket, remembering nothing.
And when it comes time for a silhouette
to throw an invented shadow
before a train, thought throws shadow across shadow.

Lamp

The night has added a silo
and companions descend from the sky
or rather are lowered
into position. For waking must be absorbed by our heirs
until there no longer remains
a charter or reconciliation
we would like as a reward. The door
of the shed opens.
The door of the tavern opens.
We are on trial considering the scrupulous
floating wheat.

Crown

The night has added a fable
told by some descending candor.
The best and the worst coming ashore.
Returning no answer at all, an altitude of waxy shapes
with eyes like sequins
swim through a lustrous Prussian blue—
a tabloid. The world is saturated.
Here is the hedgerow, proving the infancy
and helplessness of our car,
reeling inconsolably beyond the land.

Objects Which Are Final

Like the hill placed before us, large and entire,
growing as our car draws toward upstate New York,
the issues become simplified: color versus drawing:
trees in autumn versus trees in winter;
one begins to find key terms in nature.
The commonplace is filled with central ideas.
Farms are there, and cities
that have come down from the mountains.
Earlier and farther east men traveled to their farms,
returning at night to a high place where they were protected
and where their leisure had range.
There they are,
gathering in the sky, passing the time
convivially, until dawn
requires they recede into chores.

The hill isolated
so that we might consider its sturdy, terrestrial beauty
and draw close. Our car moves us
while we, *who strain in spirit to capture*
the magnificence of strength, also are approaching,
praising each translation
that shifts the hill *and space to breathe,*
the ride unrolling a victory
celebration. All earth is the topic:
the mountain, the hill, the plateau, the plain—
nature's rhetorical forms.
Accomplished in one of them,
we all of a sudden believe in finality,
though it pass beyond the windshield,
the delayed crown of the ode falling
to us, as victory falls next to the ones coming up—
as Pindar was wont to remind them.

Passed on, donated, or given
away to those crowding trees of all nationalities.

They grow up, entwined
or standing shoulder-to-shoulder,
closely following the escarpment. We look at the road,
seeing them obliquely, letting them stream
red, green, yellow, blue.

Historic Site

Dissolved in the distance
a wife or pale landscape behind the equestrian
is like imagination, and he pointing back
explains her. You can see an era in them, perhaps what is meant
by ethos. It is one of the lost scenes
like a niche in a wall

or a small news item: she stood on a terrace
and heard amplified trees "as chilling as the tombs themselves."

But sensation does not account for the whole thing.
Within the stifling text, a quarrel underlines
the lack of proficiency two men will have tomorrow,
and you admire the construction that makes you think this.

You reenter the disputed space considering a vestibule
whose pilasters taper down
and whose stairs double and redouble
so that climbing is thick and impossibly mournful
even as you say under breath that you can teach
since you've done it before,
and you continue to be aware of this plane
while the men are recovering, pitifully boisterous.
A sudden depth passed around

in the news already fallen beneath troop momentum
or the peasants
stumbling in is vengeful yet adoring like overgrown masses of bushes.

Profusion is followed by civil war
with little space between, a portion
you barely stand on.

Greenhouses and Gardens

Of the hunted rabbit, strangely and undramatically put into,
and who fell into the crib of flowers like the pelt
of the hero. It took remarkable sensibility
to place his death in a garden, letting the accidental victim
fall as if it fit him into the least statistically likely bed.

When Breton describes Arshile's remembering
it suspiciously sounds like
remembering for him. This should be checked.
Gorky always exaggerated his states of feeling,
the heat, the tenderness, the edible, the lusciousness, the song—
an imitation oriental carpet.
I was looking at it when I realized his colors suspend in the same way,
in a solvent, permissive yet starved.

I am reading letters translated from the Armenian.
The language is secluded. Writing to the person
who is his sister he can speak
of his provincial memories, *the heat, the tenderness* . . .
The extortionist grows less.

Dearest beloveds, recall father's garden
of apricots and ruins where we used to play,
the shrine, the milled wheat
down the path from our house,
and the morose clocks
of Ararat or Mont Sainte-Victoire,
and the Tree of the Cross upon which the authentic,
although sometimes suspicious and proud crane,
white where he flew, was absent when
Armenian villagers attached the colorful
pennants of their clothing.

His letters rendered the biography I had read atmospheric,
bluish. Distant access.
As if the writer were permitted to read only press releases.
A generation of writers is embarrassed.

The bland composite photo they posted is embarrassing:
his letters show real criminality.
Clearly he did not let them through but entertained them
in the tavern or on calling cards,
in places where "social privacy" is.
The same hand that really is the immigrant
carries the pose, perhaps even to his sister.
Perhaps, like everything else, primary sources are premeditated:

the episodic hills,
the credentials of nature with which he covered himself,
where seed pods like small glass bottles of cologne
absorbed him and his faith and went into
his meeting with Breton—
who in the introduction to the catalogue
said his forms are analogical—
gradually nature taking on protective coloring.
Meanwhile he pleads to be accepted the way he is.

Personal letters are like a greenhouse.
They step into the garden to have a word with you.
They speak, they touch your arm.
You vow to go away together.
The extravagant humidity lasts from cover to cover,
and personality is palpable.
They touch upon the situation.

Gaze, Blunder

A courtyard awaits us
at every turn, spoken or unspoken. A public garden
for when either of us is not at home,
or as a penalty for intimacy,
suggests itself and then is propped up in the heart,
like a cut from a record.
The spring comes, popular as ever.
Why do you say that? I feel unprotected
and desperate, returning to the subject again
and again, while the car pulls away from the approach lane
into traffic as if it had all been arranged beforehand.
A garden with a grove of trees, sensing
the time of day,
is answered by a sundial and a pair of reflecting pools
under the sky. Our comportment
is fluctuating now that we have exchanged places,
and at the entrance to the conservatory are two
reflecting pools and a sundial
surrounded by walking and accompanied by the length of the plateau
where the two reflecting pools are, as we go downstairs
to the parking lot.
I feel like an amateur in a dream
overpowered by the course that speaks.
Farther down, the accordionist is overpowering
the circumstance of his being there,
a pale orbit of passersby.
We are conversant with his false and strong abundance.
Some stars, lowering their gaze, walk away.
One need only look at them trying to button their coats
as they return to the piercing world.

Inscription

"Get out of my sight," he said, "the further, the better."
An uncharitable wind seems final.
Every day we add something to our withdrawal
like a weapon which flies blindly and unthinkingly
to its mark, and we are similarly seized with the desire
to probe an earlier version of ourselves
now that it is foreign. Today we have added the tendency
to exaggerate, to commemorate new damages, each containing
its own god. In this, as in other matters,
removing ourselves is impossible: the barge has already
proceeded to begin the serious process
of dropping boulders into the water,
and from its lap will fall an island of almost protective delicacy.

Sleepless Before Sleep

The smoke clears, and whatever needs to be composed
is put away. "Restore the same
innocence for your friends, too"
is one among many petitioning voices.
But it is essential that the woman be convicted
no matter how unwilling her accuser,
and since the indecipherable logic that follows her
is especially charismatic in public places
she chooses home. Foxes have holes,
birds of the air have nests.
By "home" is understood "descent,"
the wedding of the blank and the slow
with the anonymity our faces knew in only one direction,
a low barrier separated from the world.
Also present is someone who says he knows her, who asks
to be remembered to the daughter and the sons
who used to occupy his summer house.
This is the liberal dream of all of us,
and so the body perpetually responds,
assumes the wish of another and grows flushed.
The meaning of her existence has already
been most adequately expressed. Innocent or not,
her dress is caught on something.